# KARMA MANUAL

The ornamental, stylized depictions of Ganesh that introduce each chapter are from the Indian Vijay font produced and copyrighted by Vijay Patel.

Ganesh is the omnipresent, living reality in every facet of Hindu life, the patron of Indian mathematics and numerology, through which can be understood the ultimate principles of the manifest Universe. The elephant-headed deity is the keeper of the Akashic records, and is usually shown riding on or above a mouse, his vehicle, which can slip easily into the most hidden and obscure corners.

*For every action, there is an equal and*
*opposite reaction.*

— Sir Isaac Newton

This is the essence of Karma—that all thoughts, emotions, and actions have an inevitable consequence. Karma is a basic doctrine in which nothing is pre-ordained; rather, everything unfolds logically from what has preceded it. Further, its principles are universal; an understanding of Karma does not require adherence to any particular religious belief or dogma.

Four types of Karma affect our lives: SaBija Karma (brought into this life), Agami Karma (acquired in this life), Prarabdha Karma (currently being played out), and Dridha Karma (the inevitable). By studying the principles of Karma and Cosmic Law, we can learn to reverse the effects of negative Karma and experience fuller, happier lives.

Written with the Western student in mind, this book is part lecture and part working journal, highlighted by anecdotal stories and inspiring quotes. *Karma Manual* will guide you through the "Karma Processing Factory," a powerful technique for gaining insight into yourself and bringing about release and transformation. Finally, the specialized Nine-Day Karma cleansing program, *Karma Shakti Kriya,* is designed to help dissolve certain types of Karma and promote individual spiritual evolution.

# About the Author

Dr. Jonn Mumford, D.O., D.C. (Swami Anandakapila Sara-swati), is a direct disciple of Dr. Swami Gitananda of South India, and Paramahansa Swami Satyananda Saraswati of Bihar, India, by whom he was initiated in 1973. Dr. Mumford is respected across the world for his knowledge and scholarship. He frequently lectures on relaxation techniques, sexuality, Tantra, and other aspects of human development and spirituality.

Dr. Mumford is a world-renowned authority on Tantra and yoga. During the 1970s he frequently demonstrated cardiac cessation, obliteration of pulse beat at will, sensory withdrawal, voluntary breath retention over the five-minute range, and start and stop bleeding on command.

His background combines years of experience as a physician with extensive international experience in a wide range of Eastern disciplines, making Dr. Mumford eminently well suited to the task of disseminating the secrets of Tantra to the West. He divides his time between South India, the United States, and Australia.

Home page:  HYPERLINK, http://www.YogaMagik.com
e-mail: jonn@yogamagik.com

# To Write to the Author

If you wish to contact the author or would like more information about this book, please write to the author in care of Llewellyn Worldwide, and we will forward your request. Both the author and publisher appreciate hearing from you and learning of your enjoyment of this book and how it has helped you. Llewellyn Worldwide cannot guarantee that every letter written to the author will be answered, but all will be forwarded. Please write to:

Dr. Jonn Mumford, D.C., D.O.
Llewellyn Worldwide Ltd.
P.O. Box 64383, Dept. K490–1, St. Paul, MN 55164-0383, U.S.A.
Please enclose a self-addressed, stamped envelope for reply, or $1.00 to cover costs.  If outside U.S.A., enclose international postal reply coupon.

*9 Days to Change Your Life*

# KARMA MANUAL

## DR. JONN MUMFORD

*(Swami Anandakapila Saraswati)*

with Meghan Stevens

2001
Llewellyn Publications
St. Paul, Minnesota, 55164-0383, U.S.A.

FIRST EDITION
Second Printing, 2001

Co-author: Meghan Stevens
Cover design by Lisa Novak
Editing and interior design by Connie Hill

Library of Congress Cataloging-in-Publication Data
Mumford, Jonn
    Karma manual: 9 days to change your life /
Jonn Mumford with Meghan Stevens. — 1st ed.
        p.    cm.
    Includes bibliographical references and index.
    ISBN 1–56718–490–1
        1. Karma.   2. Spiritual life.   3. Hinduism—Doctrines.
I. Stevens, Meghan.    II. Title.
BL2015.K3M86        1999
294.5'22—dc21                                          99-20742
                                                          CIP

Llewellyn Publications
A Division of Llewellyn Worldwide, Ltd.
P.O. Box 64383, Dept. K490–1
St. Paul, Minnesota 55164-0383, U.S.A.
www.llewellyn.com

Printed in the United States of America
on recycled paper

Dedicated to the memory of
Yogarishi Dr. Swami Gitananda Giri
Yoga Samadhi 2:20 A.M., December 29, 1993

*Om Namah Shiva*

# Other Books by Dr. Jonn Mumford

*Ecstasy Through Tantra* (1987)

*A Chakra & Kundalini Workbook* (1994)

*Magical Tattwa Cards: A Complete System for Self-Development* (1997)

*Mind Magic Kit* (1998)

*Death: Beginning or End?* (1999)

*Psychosomatic Yoga* (Thorson's, 1974)

# Contents

# FOREWORD

 This book is an explanation of the complex topic of Karma and its ramifications as expounded by a contemporary Western Master, Dr. Jonn Mumford (Swami Anandakapila Saraswati).

Working on this book has been a most enjoyable and beneficial experience. While doing so I have experienced several profound realizations. I hope you also experience this as you read it.

The material presented here evolved from a live lecture to students, recorded in 1987 at Westgate House, Dr. Jonn Mumford's Ashram in Sydney, Australia. The lecture was titled "Karma: Yours or Mine? Ours!" This book contains much additional material that enhances the esoteric understanding of Karma, and a special emphasis is placed on practical aspects for Western students.

Jonn Mumford (Swami Anandakapila Saraswati) has lived and studied in India. He was initiated by Yogarishi Dr. Swami Gitananda Giri and also by Paramahansa Satyananda Saraswati into a monastic order established in A.D. 800. He now lectures and teaches in Sydney, Australia.

See Dr. Mumford's Internet Home Page at:

**http: //www.ozemail.com.au/~mumford8**

for more information about Dr. Mumford, the Yoga Magik International Course, and the Yantra Philosophic Society.

— Meghan Cheryl Stevens
Managing Director, YogaMagik
Sydney, NSW, Australia
1997

# ACKNOWLEDGMENTS

 I am deeply grateful to Mrs. Verna Fielding, Eastern School of Yoga, Melbourne, Australia for her immense effort in transcribing the original tape lectures on which this manual is based.

My gratitude to Mr. Ricky Dean Kawulia for his keen eye, expert proofreading, and advice.

I would like to thank Penguin Books U.K. for gracious permission to quote from Hart Defouw and Robert Svoboda's *Light On Life: An Introduction to the Astrology of India* (Penguin Books) and Robert Svoboda's *Ayurveda; Life, Health and Longevity* (Penguin Books)

A profound thank you to the Llewellyn Publications staff and in particular, Connie Hill, Senior Editor, for her untiring efforts in the editing, design, and production of this book.

Finally this book would not have existed without the vision, efforts, encouragement, and persistence of my co-author, Meghan Stevens, Managing Director, Yoga-Magik. It was she who first saw the possibility of the present volume.

# INTRODUCTION

I have designed this book as a practical working manual, by a Westerner for Westerners. In no sense is this work intended to be an academic discussion of Karma. There is a surfeit of such texts, mostly of interest to Indologists and deeply committed students of traditional Hindu and Yoga philosophy.

My object is to make the subject of Karma, and as a secondary consideration Dharma, accessible to the Western reader. I do not find it possible to discuss life in a meaningful and wholistic way without utilizing the concepts of "action and reaction," "duty," and "reincarnation." Such topics are not, for me, simply a matter of belief or faith, but rather a principle of necessity and mental hygiene.

Dr. Elmer Green of the Menninger clinic, used the term "Biofeedback: Yoga of the West." When dealing with the doctrine of Karma for Westerners, I have adapted a procedure that might be summed up as "Psychotherapy: Yoga of the West."

Each chapter ends with a special procedure I call the "Karma Processing Factory." This form of Western Gnana Yoga brings about release through *understanding* aspects of the personal self. The technique works at a deep unconscious level and can be quite transformative.

The final chapter gives the Nine-Day Karma Shakti Kriya, which is a jewel of Dr. Swami Gitananda's teaching that he bequeathed to me.

One of the first people to present Karma for the English-speaking public in an understandable way was the founder of the American Rosicrucian Order (AMORC), Dr. H. Spencer Lewis. His son, Ralph M. Lewis, who is slowly being recognized as a truly American philosopher, amplified his groundbreaking work.

This book is intended to provide a clear, simple and fast practical guide to the topic of Karma. I have attempted to explain the teachings in an understandable Western context, combined with the traditional, and yet innovative, approach of my first Guru, Dr. Swami Gitananda Giri of Tamil Nadu, South India.

— Dr. Jonn Mumford
Sydney, NSW, Australia
1997

# 1
# KARMA: YOURS OR MINE? OURS!

 ## Cosmic Law

Karma is a key that we may use to organize our lives, rather than endlessly agonizing over the seemingly unexplainable and often unexpected events forming the fabric of our lives.

The subject of Karma is basic to all of us and this doctrine, first fully expounded in Hindu and Buddhist philosophy, is the secret to resolving many apparent mysteries.

Albert Einstein said "God does not play dice with the Universe." It is only through understanding Karma, which does not need a personal theistic view of a God, that we can even begin to make sense of Einstein's statement.

Karma is not about fate, fatalism, or destiny; nothing is pre-ordained—rather everything is a sequential happening emerging logically from antecedents. Karma is a way of viewing existence that brings about a harmony of both *fatalism* and *free will,* resulting in increased mental health and self-responsibility.

**The holistic doctrine of Karma gives us a reason for everything and everything for a reason. Karma, as a philosophy, maintains hope in the midst of hopelessness and provides us with the courage to continue our personal evolution.**

Karma has nothing to do with concepts of God's judgment, punishment, pain, or penalty. Nor is it a simplistic "eye for an eye; tooth for a tooth" creed.

Karma is not about *sin*, original or otherwise, except possibly in the sense of the Greek word that was translated into the English word "sin" in the King James Bible. The Greek word translated as "sin" meant to "miss the mark," and was an archer's term for not hitting the target.

Each of us, if we accept an ultimate purpose of self-realization, may find it useful to regularly appraise if we are hitting the *target* or *sinning* by missing the mark?

In the New Testament, the Apostle Paul echoed a sentiment perhaps reminiscent of Karma and ultimate spiritual goals when he wrote:

> 6:7  Be not deceived: God is not mocked: for whatsoever a man soweth, that shall he also reap.
>
> 6:8  For he that soweth to his flesh shall of the flesh reap corruption; but he that soweth to the Spirit shall of the Spirit reap life everlasting.
>
> 6:9  And let us not be weary in well doing: for in due season we shall reap, if we faint not.
>
> — *Galatians*, Chapter 6

I am not asking you to believe anything discussed here, nor am I interested in interfering with your belief system. I believe in no deity, no institution, and no religion. I believe in only two categories; one of those categories is the ever-present altruistic potential of human beings. I believe in myself as a human, and I believe in other human beings.

The second category that I believe in has to do with *Universal Law*—cosmic teachings that have their origin in Hindu and Buddhist Philosophy. These laws are consequences that exist independently and have nothing to do with religion or *churchianity*. They have nothing to do with institutions or even with Hinduism and Buddhism, although they are deeply embedded within those concepts. These are the only two things that I have any belief in, any faith in whatsoever: *human beings* and *cosmic laws*.

The primary cosmic laws are called Karma and Dharma.

> *Karma is the law of*
> *psycho-spiritual growth that*
> *involves an equal and opposite*
> *reaction for every action.*
> *Karma is a process designed*
> *to ensure evolution*
> *of consciousness.*

Many of you will be familiar with the concept of Karma or at least the word. I want to explore the topic of Karma in a simple and useful way and to comment on the choices or options we have when we examine Karma as a fundamental law.

> *Dharma is the inherent*
> *individual responsibility each of*
> *us owes to (1) the society of*
> *sentient beings we are born*
> *into, (2) the environment,*
> *and finally, (3) the*
> *higher "self" within us.*

The Hindu accepts that Dharma, or duty, is an inescapable part of living. As Dr. Swami Gitananda Giri said: "Life owes us nothing—we have already been given the gift of life—and it is we who owe everything to the world and the community."

He or she who wastes life commits spiritual suicide—we all have a Dharma or duty to further group evolution and personal development by the very act of being alive!

In South Indian numerology, as taught by Dr. Swami Gitananda, the very date and time of your birth gives you a clue concerning your *Dharma Marga*.

When we are born, not only do we have a collective Dharma to the community at large, but also we have a personal Dharma or *Swadharma*. Herein lies a tale, because the biggest single cause of frustration and unhappiness is the *failure to fulfill your own Swadharma*.

Swadharma has to do with one's own innate psychic tendency or nature and what is precisely required for one's growth. Better to do your own Swadharma than another's Dharma. It has been stated that growth comes from acting according to that which is natural for you, and fulfilling Swadharma represents the only known method of achieving satisfaction and joy.

This is such a lesson that I could not emphasize it enough and can only end by quoting from an interview with Sir Francis Chichester, the first man to sail solo around the world. In May 1967 he sailed into Sydney harbor on the final lap of his record-breaking voyage.

One does these things because one has a
certain nature. One cannot get away from fate.
　　If a person does not fulfill his nature, he
will lead a frustrated life and be unhappy.
　　If it involves him in fear he will just have
to put up with it.
　　　　　　　　　　　— Sir Francis Chichester

I will give you a very practical approach to *processing*
your personal Karma and finally a very direct method
for using a "Nine-Day Karma Clearing Program" (chapter 12).

I am going to tell you a great many stories, some of
them pleasant, some of them not so pleasant. All of the
stories will be instructive and are designed to impact
and shift deep psychic layers within you. Let me begin
with a story about a scorpion and a turtle.

# The Scorpion and the Turtle

The scorpion and the turtle met by a riverbank. In a certain sense that river is like the river of life—we all seek a
raft to cross over that river of life.

The scorpion said to the turtle, "Will you carry me
across on your back to the other side?" The turtle
looked at the scorpion and said "No! I've heard about
you scorpions. You scorpions are impulsive, you are
sociopathic, you are unpredictable. It would be just like
you, as a scorpion, to sting me, and I would drown."

And the scorpion replied, "My dear fellow, just use
simple common sense, use logic—if I were to sting you

would that make sense? You would drown and I would drown—we both would end up very dead!"

The turtle considered the scorpion's words and thought: that's right, he can't afford to sting me, so why not ferry him across on my back? "All right, hop on my back," said the turtle.

The pair started off across the river, and sure enough, halfway across the river the scorpion stung the turtle, and the turtle started to die of the poison. They began to drown and were both gulping water, going down and coming up. The turtle screamed at the scorpion, "What did you do this for? It doesn't make sense!"

And the scorpion replied: *"Life doesn't make sense!"*

# Philosophy of Karma

That is exactly the position that we are interested in— each one of us is concerned with the question of meaning in life. Somewhere along the line we have to make a choice—is there a sense to life, or is life made up of nonsense?

Some of you perhaps are not aware that I was initiated and trained in India. I do not teach what we call in Hindi, *Katab Yoga*. Katab means "book" Yoga. I write books but my Yoga doesn't come out of books, and my initiated name is Anandakapila.

Kapila was a contemporary of Buddha and the founder of Samkhya, one of the six classical schools of Indian philosophy. Kapila was a man, like Buddha, who sat down and thought about the universe and life. Did existence have meaning or was it meaningless? Did it have sense or was it nonsensical? As a result of his contemplation, Kapila developed a system of understanding that brought into focus the Laws of the Universe, including Karma.

Since most of you are interested in Yoga, let me tell you that Samkhya and Yoga go together like a horse and a cart, a boy and a girl, night and day. Samkhya is the theoretical basis on which the practice of Yoga rests. It is sufficient to state that a cornerstone of Samkhya, of Hinduism, and of Buddhism in general, is the concept of Karma.

You and I as human beings are very funny people. If we hear about a concept such as Karma we set up an automatic projection mechanism; we assume because Karma is a doctrine that teaches "for every action there is an equal and opposite reaction," therefore it must be something that happens only to other people.

A precise definition would emphasize that every action has an inevitable consequence—that there is no activity, be it mental or emotional, or simply a physical observable action in the world, from which there is no resulting consequence.

Karma is, if you wish, a psychic equivalent of Newton's theory of action and reaction. It is the psychic equivalent of Newtonian physics, for as far as you push in one direction, the pendulum is going to swing back an equal arc on the other side. Karma in essence is a principle that for every turn of the mind-body complex and every action in the external world, there must be an inevitable consequence.

> ***Karma is to psychics as Newton's Third Law of Motion is to physics: "Whenever one object exerts a force on a second object, the second exerts an equal and opposite force on the first."***

Or a slightly more formal statement of the Third Law of Motion:

> Action and reaction are equal and opposite,
> i.e. when two bodies interact the force
> exerted by the first body on the second body
> is equal and opposite to the force exerted by
> the second body on the first.
> — Newton's *Principia*, 1687
> (from *Chambers Science & Technology Dictionary*)

Newton's First and Second laws of Motion also are occult paradigms about personal and spiritual growth:

> ***I. Every body (everybody) continues in a state of rest or uniform motion in a straight line unless acted upon by an external impressed force.***
> (Translation: If you keep on doing what you have been doing, you are going to keep on

getting what you have been getting—someone
pointed out that to imagine otherwise is a
very fine definition of "Insanity"!)

**II. The rate of change of momentum is propor-
tional to the impressed force and takes place in
the direction of the force.** (Translation: *"God
helps those who help themselves"* and it is worth
considering *"if you can't beat them join them,"*
or in new age parlance *"go with the flow!"*)

All of us, as human beings, are in a very peculiar situation, because somehow it is *always somebody else's
Karma.* We very seldom think about it in relationship
to ourselves. Or at least I will speak for myself—I prefer
not to think about it. Unfortunately I have been
trained so I can't avoid the issue, but it is always somebody else's Karma—we have this automatic projection
mechanism.

It is like two fellows who at midnight are both quite
drunk. One turns to the other and says, "You are too
drunk to drive—when I look at you, your face is
blurred." Psychologists call that projection.

We have this kind of projection attitude—it is always
someone else's Karma. As an example: you are actually
wasting your time if you complain. It is a verifiable
observation that when you talk to people about your
problems, fifty percent of them are not interested, and
the other fifty percent are glad you are getting what's
coming to you.

*For most of us,
Karma is something
that happens
to someone else!*

The fact is that Karma is a Universal Law. It represents a tremendous web or weave in which there is an eternal series of action and reaction, of push and pull, of interplay in which all of our lives are bound up.

## What Is this Book About?

I propose to look at the doctrine of Karma and amplify it. This is no small feat because it could go on indefinitely, but it will not. I want to examine according to the classical teachings of Karma, to comment on Karma generally, and to talk about the Bhagavad Gita, which is a textbook of Karma Yoga.

I am concerned with employing simply and directly whatever mechanisms are useful for Europeans, and consequently we will have a Karma *processing* exercise at the end of each chapter, and finally a whole chapter devoted to clearing your personal Karma.

A comment is necessary about the "Karma Processing Factory" techniques at the end of each chapter. These techniques are very powerful when taken individually and seriously worked on. They are based on *Life Script* questionnaires developed by Dr. Eric Berne's Transactional Psychology movement many years ago. At that time, in the 1970s, I belonged to an initial group of Australians who first trained, under the auspices of the Public Health department, in Gestalt techniques and Transactional theory.

I have transformed and developed the underrated "Life-Script" questionnaire into a totally powerful system of individual psychotherapy, and spent many years practicing with the methods I crystallized. A portion of that labor is presented in this book for your use.

I strongly recommend that at the end of each chapter you use a pencil and eraser to work through each exercise; this is a powerful method of gaining insight into yourself, clearing out unwanted automatic actions, and thus lessening the amount and rate at which new Karma accumulates.

In the last chapter I am going to teach you a routine called the *Karma Shakti Kriya,* a nine-day routine that helps to dissolve certain types of Karma. My first Guru, Dr. Swami Gitananda Giri, taught this program to me in 1958.

Finally I want to give you a comment, when we have put it all together—as much as we can put such a vast subject together—a comment about what could possibly happen with the information.

# Karma Processing Factory: Assembly Line One

## *"Who am I?"*

The most important question asked in Vedanta is "Ko Ham"; "Who Am I?" Swami Gitananda was fond of telling the story about the Buddha Sattva who traveled to China and established the schools that later would emerge as Zen in Japan—and he often said that the Sanskrit word *Ko Ham* became Zen Buddhism's *Koan*.

A Koan is a conundrum in the form of a question that can only be solved outside the realm of logic, e.g. "what is the sound of one hand clapping?"

The Emperor of China called the Buddha Sattva to the Imperial Court and asked him: "Who are you?"

"I haven't the faintest idea," replied the Buddha Sattva, and promptly walked out of the court. We are told that the Buddha Sattva spent the next twenty years meditating upon "Ko Ham."

So now I am going to suggest that you take a pencil and very seriously work on the question "Ko Ham," i.e. "Who am I?" and not in a superficial or pseudo-spiritual intellectual way.

*"Who am I?"* is not a new age query to answer by filling up the page with "I am a child of God, divinity is in my being, I am continuing and becoming more sentient and compassionate as a result of my last incarnation as Napoleon," etc., and other such drivel!

*"Who am I?"* is also not intended as a bit of superficial biodata: e.g., "I was born in 1936 at a hospital in New York. I am 5'9" with black hair, brown eyes, and false teeth"—you and five million other people! Such data really says nothing about "you" and your feelings, aspirations, likes, dislikes, feelings of adequacy and inadequacy, viewpoints about life, etc.

Consider the thoughtful and revealing comments to this question that I garnered from patients during the years I ran the Rose Bay Counseling Center.

Comments from others :

> Describe yourself: *"I am a career woman, I am unfeminine, hate domesticity, but am house proud, I like honesty and realism and I prefer directness. I am nothing developing into something. I love fun, but don't want to age mentally."*
>
> — Female, thirty-eight, married, three children working as an interior decorator

> Describe yourself: *"Thin, frail, scared, weathered. I see my potential but feel like sap running out in a dying plant. My mother told me I nearly killed her at birth. I always felt guilty about being born."*
>
> — Male, twenty-eight, industrial cleaner, suffering depression and social phobia

Notice how we are gripped immediately by *real* people expressing and sharing *real* feelings!

It really does not matter to us what age these fellow humans are, or their occupation—such bits of biodata fade into insignificance when placed alongside the rawness and courage of their self-statements.

So take the whole page and seriously contemplate and write down *who you are!* People often die without having ever considered "Who am I?" during their whole life, and suddenly it is too late!

*Socrates said:*
*"The unexamined life is not*
*worth living."*

# Assembly Line One: Process One

## *"Who am I?"*

Describe yourself:

*Meditation Focus*

There is no such thing as chance; and what
seems to us the merest accident springs from
the deepest source of destiny.

— Friedrich Schiller, 1759–1805

## 2
# WHAT IS KARMA?

 ## Meanings of Karma

Let's go back to Karma itself, and I will define the word for you. It comes from the Sanskrit root word, *kri*. As a noun, it is more correctly "Karman." In Sanskrit, the word literally means a ritual, an act, word, performance, or ceremony—and *ceremony* is a particularly useful concept.

The English word "ceremony" comes originally from the Sanskrit root *kri,* and ceremony is a cognate concept to Karma. For example, you go into a church and the priest performs a mass; that mass represents a ceremony. From the etymological roots of the word ceremony, we could actually call it *karmamony*.

The mass is an instance of a ceremony that is a Kar-mamony, because Karma is the doctrine that every action has an inevitable consequence, therefore a proper ceremony is a series of actions which are so designed that the outcome, which is inevitable, will be correct.

This is the real meaning of a ceremony: a series of actions that guarantee that the outcome is correct. That is the meaning of a mass, which is the meaning of all Puja or worship. Altering Karma is often the primary function of ritual in all religions and all systems of inner growth. The secondary function of ceremony is to alter your state of consciousness in a shift from the mundane to the arcane—the gross to the subtle. Let me reiterate this by quoting from my book *Ecstasy Through Tantra* (St. Paul: Llewellyn Publications, 1987):

> The words rite and right are semantic cousins.
> The truth of ritual significance may be revealed
> at a deeper level when we realize that the Eng-
> lish word "ritual" (hence "rite") etymologically
> derives from the Sanskrit prefix *RI:* "to flow
> with or away with." Indeed the value of a
> ritual or ceremony becomes even more evident
> when we know that the etymological root of
> "ceremony" is also Sanskrit—literally
> *Karmamony*, i.e. the doctrine that every action
> has a consequence and therefore the value of
> careful and correct ceremony is to ensure the
> consequences of the activity are benign.

From the root: kri, comes a word that many of you are familiar with: *Kriya,* one of the specialties of my school. Kriya and Karma both emerge from the same root. Just as ceremony is really karmamony, the word Kriya comes from the Sanskrit root *kri,* so the English word "creative" can be tracked etymologically back to the word Kriya. Kriya usually means "technique" or "action," and in English we actually recognize the concept of being creative, of releasing our personal creativity.

This tells us something: that Karma, or the Law of Karma, is an opportunity to make our lives one creative journey from womb to tomb. In fact Karma is not destiny, Karma is also free will, and in a sense it is up to us. This thing, which is not a *thing*—Karma—is subtle! You can't exactly reach out and grab a piece of karma, you can't nail a piece of Karma up on the wall—it is something subtle, so subtle that, in fact, we would describe the law of Karma as a process.

## Mechanism versus Process

Some of you may be particularly interested in the English language. At one time I was doing an applied science degree and the particular college decided that they were graduating too many people with science degrees who were illiterate, who couldn't write reports. So the faculty, in its wisdom—and they were actually very wise indeed—decided that they would have a special course in technical writing and communication so that their graduates would not be so illiterate, as engineers and scientists often appear to be, and seem to be in practice.

One of the things we learned very thoroughly during this course is that in technical writing and communication there is a distinct difference between a process and a mechanism. They are not the same thing, and I will tell you that Karma is a subtle law; it is not a mechanism, but rather a *process*.

The difference between a *mechanism* and a *process* is that *a mechanism exists in three dimensions of space and one of time*; it is something tangible, a concrete object composed often of several parts. A hypodermic syringe, for instance, is a mechanism delivering fluids into the body or aspirating fluids out of the body.

The proper definition of a process is *a sequence of actions* leading to a unit of work or a result. In no way can you actually grasp a process, because it is made up of a series of actions. Yawning, for example is a *process*.

I say this because what we are talking about is so subtle that we must understand, from the outset, that Karma is a *process*. Karma is not a mechanism, something that you can grab, any more than you can grab a yawn. A yawn is a result of a whole series of actions that lead to a result. Yes, you can see the end result, which is the yawn, but you can't exactly grab the yawn—it is a *process*, and *Karma* is also a process.

## Hindu Philosophy

In Hindu Philosophy it was observed that if there was to be any sense in life, if a person was to have any control of his destiny and in turn to be answerable to self, then time and again this subtle process of Karma showed up.

*Karma, as a doctrine, is the recognition of the fundamental laws of action and reaction within the human nervous system. It is a sophisticated overview of Western psychology's "Stimulus— Black Box—Response arc."*
— *A Chakra & Kundalini Workbook*

## Categories of Karma

In the classical teachings, particularly as clarified in the eighth century A.D. by Hindu reformer Shankacharya, Karma was divided into three categories. There are many other subdivisions, but three primary categories of Karma are of major importance.

These three categories of Karma are: *SaBija Karma, Agami Karma,* and *Parabdhra Karma.*

The first type of Karma has also been designated as *Sancheet Karma.* The name I prefer, because it is more self-explanatory, is SaBija Karma.

The prefix *Sa* in Sanskrit means "with," and Bija means "a seed." SaBija Karma is the Karma with which we are born that has resulted from prior lives.

> *The seeds of destiny already stored as a result of former lives, but which have not yet begun to germinate . . . . they have not yet begun to sprout, mature, and transform themselves into the harvest of a life.*
> — Heinrich Zimmer,
> *Philosophies of India*

Note that at the beginning I said distinctly that I am not interested in altering your belief system. You may or may not agree with the concept of life after life, an endless cycle of birth and death and rebirth, but it doesn't matter whether you believe in it or not; that is of no consequence.

Half the world's population believes in the doctrine of Samsara: the eternal bondage of rebirth, the cycle of life and death. Buddhists, Hindus, and offshoots of Buddhism and Hinduism and Esoteric teachings in the West *all agree on this*. Consequently, reincarnation has become a formal doctrine accepted by half the population of this planet.

I will make a suggestion to you, which you do not have to believe, that the teaching of life after life may or may not be so, and I would suggest to you that the belief that it is so is also an esoteric teaching. There is an outer teaching, and by my understanding, as my Gurus have taught me, there is also an inner or esoteric meaning to the concept of reincarnation.

I will share with you one aspect of the esoteric or inner teaching about the doctrine concerning *life after life*.

> *What does reincarnate, in endless rounds of birth after birth, is the chain of associational thinking that eternally goes on within all of us. Each thought is a birth and each cessation of the thought is a death. The tendency for us is to recycle our thoughts in ever-recurring patterns.*

The Yogi gains freedom from the wheel of rebirth by sacrificing *thinking* for *being*.

> *Yoga is the cessation of the*
> *fluctuations (thoughts)*
> *of the mind-stuff.*
> — Patanjali's *Yoga Sutras*

I also want to emphasize that everything we will study about Karma leads to a big-picture perspective that means there is no such thing as a *failed life*.

> *Life is a graduate school and*
> *the entrance prerequisite is a*
> *birth certificate: graduates are*
> *awarded a death certificate;*
> *consequently in the school of*
> *life there are no FAILURES.*
> — Anandakapila

# Karma Processing Factory: Assembly Line Two

*What do you feel or know about your birth?*
*What is your earliest memory at this moment?*

We can only deal with Karmic aspects of our lives to the degree that we can understand and recognize the psychological effects the past has upon our evolution.

Memory is defined in J. P. Chaplin's *Dictionary of Psychology* (New York: Dell, 1985) as "The function involved in reliving past experiences," an ideal definition for the Karma processing exercises in this book.

Karma processing involves dealing with Agami Karma by discovering or realizing how the dead hand of the past reaches into the present, throttling our creative life affirmations urges in the *now*.

The entrance portals to the Oracle of Delphi had emblazoned in Greek "Man know thyself," followed by the lesser-known maxim: "All things In Moderation." These two statements sum up the total Karmic and Dharmic rules for living properly, East or West.

I am going to ask you shortly to write down what you believe you know about your birth, and also the very earliest memory you can recall at this moment.

I am not talking about complicated machinations that have led to the recent epidemic tragedy of over-zealous therapists producing "False Memory syndrome," nor the crazies devoting their lives to fantasizing *ritual abuse* on every street corner. As some police chief commented: "If every story of ritual abuse had a foundation in fact, America would be one huge graveyard."

This is an extremely common-sensical and useful procedure I am going to ask you participate in—nothing to do with wild fantasies!

Consider the following examples taken from my clinical records.

Comments from others:

> What do you feel or know about your birth?
> *"Mom said no doctor or midwife was available and [she] consequently had to suppress my birth until she couldn't stand it—I am terrified of water as a result, and to this day can't put my head under water. Generally I have a very negative feeling about my birth as I was constantly reminded by my mother that my older brother was dying at the time."*
>
> — Female, eighteen, student

> What is your earliest memory at this moment?
> *"Playing in streets about age four, and being bullied and teased by Australian kids because I could hardly speak English, and my father and mother were waps (Australian slang for Italians)."*
>
> — Male, forty, married with three children, builder

What is your earliest memory at this moment? *"Old stained glass windows and a wooden floor at about four years of age. Eating stale sandwiches at kindergarten about age five. Fracturing my leg at about seven years, and feeling guilty about the trouble it caused my mother."*

— Male, twenty-four, depressed clerk

The techniques I am giving you are *karmic catalysts,* and you will get out of them exactly what you put into them. Fill in the spaces with this self-evaluation.

# Assembly Line Two: Process One

*What do you feel or know about your birth?*

# Assembly Line Two: Process Two

*What is your earliest memory
at this moment?*

## Meditation Focus

There are only three events in a man's life:
birth, life, and death:
he is not conscious of being born,
he dies in pain,
and he forgets to live.

— Jean de la Bruyere, 1645–1696

# 3
# SABIJA KARMA

##  Seeding Karma

From my viewpoint, categorically, you are born with SaBija Karma from a prior life. One prior life that I guarantee you have had is a total existence spanning approximately nine months in duration. It started from the moment of conception and ended at birth, and is called an intrauterine existence. While you were swimming in a sea of amniotic fluid, your SaBija Karma was being laid down.

SaBija Karma is the cycle of events that happened to you in the womb and that continues to affect you after birth. It means that at the moment of birth there are seeds of Karma already within you that may or may not be sprouted. Each of us is carrying around SaBija Karma and it can be sprouted at any moment. I will tell you here how SaBija Karma becomes manifest, according to the classical teaching.

This prior life (at least the one prior life, that intrauterine existence), from the moment of conception to birth, represents a complete cycle. A complete cycle is creation, life, and death. I would suggest that for the fetus to be born, ending its intrauterine existence, is as death is for the living person.

At that moment of birth, the fetus dies to its full cycle of life within the womb, within that alchemical crucible of the uterus. During those nine months (and in classical teachings many lives before that) there is Karma laid down, which Western psychology will come to observe more and more.

*The three trimesters of pregnancy are equivalent to the agricultural sowing, cultivating, and harvesting phases, with all the attendant Karmic actions and reactions.*

The nineteenth-century English poet, Samuel Taylor Coleridge, observed:

> The history of man for the nine months preceding his birth would probably be far more interesting, and contain events of greater moment, than all the three score and ten years that follow it.

This intrauterine existence is a total life cycle of birth (conception), youth (the first trimester as an embryo), adulthood (the second trimester transition into fetus, with five senses and genitals developed) and finally senescence with approaching death (the third trimester, terminating in birth).

Biologist Lyall Watson comments in his book *Beyond Supernature* (New York: Bantam, 1988): "The infant knows it must be born, just as we know we must die! Birth to an infant is as death to us."

He goes on to say: "The most hazardous journey we ever make is down 4 inches of birth canal propelled with a force sufficient to break an obstetrician's finger."

It is an Indian tradition, as well as a belief of many ancient cultures, that the fetus may be influenced psychically by the mother's emotional state: this is a contemporary Rosicrucian (AMORC) teaching, and certainly the amount of psycho-physiological information received by the unborn is an overwhelming equivalent to the later sensate experiences of life.

As early as 1948, the *Journal of Experimental Psychology* had established that at five months the fetus could accurately distinguish sounds in terms of pitch and tone. It is now possible to insert miniature microphones into the pregnant uterus, establishing the fact that the fetus is floating in an underwater sound studio with acoustic vibrations being tremendously magnified.

## Sprouting Karma

So already, by that act of being born, Karma is seeded within us. How is this Karma sprouted?

Generally a seed will not grow if it is kept in the desert. The only way to get a seed to sprout is to provide it with water. The SaBija Karma that is locked within each one of us is rather like a seed, and the water that sprouts it is *emotion.*

Some SaBija Karma has manifested for everyone, while some has not manifested. Consequently, no one can know easily what his or her SaBija Karma is. The SaBija Karma is triggered during or after birth.

*You might consider SaBija Karma as a psychic equivalent to genetics or nature. SaBija Karma is also reminiscent of "Teratogenic" or congenital defects, i.e. those things acquired in the womb that affect us after birth.*

The Greek root *Teras* (from which is formed Terato-genic) originally meant "a sign or portent, a monster, or *omen*," inferring that the Cosmos was signaling a message about our birth or life. In a way SaBija Karma portends our future—if only we can understand it.

SaBija Karma sprouts at any moment during your life when there is stimulus presented to you that corresponds to, or resembles, a similar stimulus that you received in the womb or at birth. The result of such a triggering can be an experience of total revulsion, with a consequent regurgitation from the depths of the nervous system and from the depths of the unconscious.

My Guru Swami Gitananda talked about SaBija Karma and how it can be triggered. We need to understand that each of us is carrying around with us SaBija Karma that may be exploded at any moment, given the right circumstances.

# A Disturbed Patient

I will tell you a true story:

Many years ago a young woman who was immensely disturbed came to me as a patient. She had broken away from her marriage and was in a deep state of despair. She had run off by herself and become involved with a fellow whose Dharma in life seemed to be that of a sociopath, or as we used to call them, a psychopath. He was a heroin addict and a thief who financed their relationship by robbing, and he was persuading her to commit robberies also.

As we talked, the girl's life began to unfold. She was one of two children. Her birth had been complicated by a very late delivery. Her mother was allowed to lie in labor for three days, and both mother and child nearly died before the child was finally born. The child actually became stuck in the birth canal.

Her father had left the family when she was two. One day the mother locked the girl, aged four years, and her three-year-old brother in the house and went away, never to be seen again. For four days that little four-year-old and her brother wandered around in the locked house desperately trying to get out, banging on windows, climbing on the door, trying to find scraps of food and water just to survive. Eventually a neighbor heard the sound of these children screaming and banging, broke a window, and got them out. Both my patient and her brother then grew up in an orphanage operated by the welfare department.

When she was eighteen or nineteen she fell in love, and she married. Her husband loved her very dearly, but he was a responsible, busy man, very concerned with his work, and was spending little time with her.

## Breaker Outers and Breaker Inners

At this point, for the psychologists here, I will tell you something very interesting. About three years ago in the United States people who were concerned with delinquent children had a new idea. These are just new ideas—people are always finding new ways of looking at things. They went to a boy's school and questioned juvenile delinquents. They found out that basically you could divide juvenile delinquents into "breaker outers," and "breaker inners." To a greater or lesser extent, all of us belong in one of these categories. We either have an impulse to break into things, places, or situations, or to break out of places or situations.

What happens is that those of us who grew up in families where we were always the odd person out, made to feel like the strange one, that others were more acceptable, are apt to go around in life trying to break into social groups or break into things.

Those of us who had very restrictive parents, with heavy judgmental opinions that they laid upon us, often escaped the family when we were young teenagers. We are consequently going around in life trying to be iconoclasts, trying to break things down and to break out, to escape marriages, jobs etc.

So, to a greater or lesser extent, we are all breaker outers or breaker inners. When you take that to the extreme, you find juvenile delinquents. They are either breaking into places or robbing and stealing cars, or running away from schools and institutions— breaking out.

## Back to the Disturbed Patient

We know that the girl's SaBija Karma was set up at birth, and this SaBija Karma is such that basically she is a breaker outer. In this marriage she had to break out; she couldn't stand the restrictions because they triggered memories of being locked in that house at age four, deserted by her mother and before that by her father, not to mention being trapped in the womb at birth.

When I saw her one day, we discussed a number of things, but I had no warning of what was about to happen, or perhaps I missed my cue! I could not foretell what was to occur. She was mixed up with this thief-cum-lover who was flying interstate, running drugs, and breaking into places to get money. One day he had a horrendous argument with her and walked out on her. He not only abandoned her, but also locked the door so she was trapped inside the apartment.

The police came around and banged on the door—she was terrified and didn't answer. They went away and within an hour she had put her head in the gas oven and killed herself. That is SaBija Karma: suddenly my patient was back in the womb, back in the house, abandoned, locked in. She was overwhelmed with an urge to break out and her entire being vomited. She committed the ultimate act of breaking out—let us hope it became a breakthrough!

## Can We Ever Know Our SaBija Karma?

Each of us is carrying our own SaBija Karma. For some of us it will contribute to our current life, for some of us it won't, but we will never know what the full extent of our SaBija Karma is. For most of us, terminal illness is

SaBija Karma—it just depends on the right time and the right circumstances. So this is one category of "Karma with seed" that you are born with—given the right conditions, the seed will sprout.

# Karma Processing Factory: Assembly Line Three

*Who was or is this person — your mother?*
*What was your mother's main comment*
*to you or her attitude to life?*

These exercises are all designed to facilitate the emergence of unconscious material from the deepest part of you. The unconscious is the feminine *womb* or alluvial soil in which the seeds of all your karma are nourished and sprouted.

Comments from others:

> Who was or is this person—your mother?
> *"Neurotic, tired, divorced, and addicted to pills;*
> *married twice. Tried to be a nice woman by*
> *helping me get what I wanted. I was her big hope*
> *in life. After fifteen I avoided her."*
>
> — Male, twenty-two, bartender, single

> Who was or is this person—your mother?
> *"She was fat and the kids always teased me*
> *about how fat she was. Distant, dreamy-eyed, no*
> *physical contact, emotional, scared of my father,*
> *afraid, conventional."*
>
> — Male, industrial cleaner

What was your mother's main comment to
you, or her attitude to life? *"You're a failure and
you will just have to make the best of it. Pull your
socks up! Wake up to yourself!"*

— Male, industrial cleaner

What was your mother's main comment to
you, or her attitude to life? *"When I first
menstruated she told me this would happen to me
once a month. Stay away from boys or you'll get
into trouble. Keep yourself clean! You are ugly,
nobody will want you."*

— Female, twenty-seven, single,
living on a psychiatric pension

You may find these examples quite disturbing
because they are very real! When you start to examine
yourself it may not be helpful to gloss over everything
and make it *nice*. However not everyone has had such
traumatic memories as the subjects I am using as
examples.

Keeping this in mind, proceed with the exercise.

# Assembly Line Three: Process One

*Who was or is this person—your mother?*

# Assembly Line Three: Process Two

*What was your mother's main comment
to you, or her attitude to life?*

*Meditation Focus*

It is interesting to consider that we may have chosen our mother carefully, from another plane and perspective, and before conception.

# 4
# AGAMI KARMA

 ## Collecting
## Agami Karma

Let me take it another step. According to Shankacharya, the second basic type of Karma is called *Agami Karma.*

Agami Karma is something you and I have been busy collecting from birth. Agami Karma is Karma that we collect during our life after birth, the result of inevitable action and reaction, or consequences to things that we have done. The seeds are there, not yet sprouted, but they can be sprouted at any moment.

*The mental and physical acts performed by an individual in the present life, the fruits of which are to be reaped in the future.*

— *A Ramakrishna-Vedanta Wordbook*

## Sprouting Agami Karma

I would suggest that by the age of nine (the Catholics say seven), the bulk of our Agami Karma has been collected, and thereafter we are just topping up. As we go through life, this Agami Karma can be fertilized and start manifesting. As a rule of thumb, the reactions in our life, both mundane and dramatic, are all examples of Agami Karma. It is easier, in theory, to find the origin of Agami Karma than SaBija Karma.

*The seeds that would normally collect and be stored if one were to continue in the path of ignorance basic to the present biography; i.e., the destiny not yet contracted.*

—Heinrich Zimmer,
*Philosophies of India*

Many years ago Dr. Swami Gitananda and I designed the schematic diagram on page 52, illustrating the principle of the Wheels ("cogs") of Karma, and how they interact. The diagram shows how an event at six years of age (Agami Karma) turns the cogs so that the consequence (or Prarabdha Karma) may be already waiting to sprout at age eighty-one, for example.

When studying this diagram you should be aware that Indian numerology teaches that our personal Karmic tides ebb and flow in ever-recurring nine-year cycles from birth. Each *Karma Yuga* is a period of nine years duration. *Yuga* means "cycle," so the term is literally "Karmic cycle."

Swamijii taught a system for detecting which phase of the nine-year cycle an individual was in at any age. In Indian numerology the number "9" is under the influence of the *martial* planet Mars, or as it is called euphemistically in Sanskrit: *Mangala*, meaning "auspicious."

The system of South Indian Numerology taught by Swamijii is studied in Sydney, Australia under the auspices of the Yantra Philosophic Society.

The method can be used to determine Karma cycles for nations, businesses, and individuals. When this is understood, the unhappy combination of karmic stages for the United States and President John F. Kennedy in the year of his assassination made such a tragedy almost unavoidable. Such Karma Yuga cycles can be plotted by the year, month, day, and even the hour.

*Often do the spirits
of great events stride on
before the events
and in today already walks
tomorrow*
— Samuel Taylor Coleridge, 1800

In 1963, the year of President Kennedy's death, the
United States was in a Karma Yuga cycle of extreme
testing. Under such a malefic influence, carelessness in
attention to details can lead to *dis-aster* (literally "the
consequences of bad stars"). The nation, in the latter
half of November, was also under an influence that
could result in adverse circumstances and a disappointment in regard to organizations, executives, and political leadership. The influence, nationally, on November
22 had to do with political activity at its most public,
and an undertonal theme of potential tragedy.

Unfortunately the man who said: "We should not let
our fears hold us back from our hopes," was under an
even more adverse influence that, combined with his
country's cycle, proved overwhelming. For John F.
Kennedy, the year 1963 was, unknown to him, a
Karmic cycle of completion—tying loose ends together,
experiencing the bitter with the sweet, and getting
ready for a new start.

For him, personally, November matched exactly the
extremely adverse cycle the United States had been

under all year, and his Karmic influences on November 22 corresponded to the nation's month cycle of political disaster.

The Karmic event that shocked the world was practically inevitable; the loss of possibly America's most loved president sank deep into the hearts of everyone. John F. Kennedy joined a long tradition of Karmic and Dharmic spiritual martyrs that include Mahatma Gandhi, Martin Luther King, Jr., Dag Hammarskjöld, and the late Prime Minister of Israel, Yitzhak Rabin, to mention only a few.

> *We are not permitted to choose the frame of our destiny. But what we put into it is ours.*
> — Dag Hammarskjöld

Fortunately such overpowering conjunctions are rare, and even if we cannot comprehend the "Why?" of such events, they nonetheless result from Karmic and Dharmic antecedents.

In attempting to come to terms with disaster and tragedy on a world scale, we need to be reminded that such occurrences produce spiritual shock waves of sensitivity in us all. Ideally, the result is an acceleration in the spiritual evolution of humanity as a whole.

# Cyclic Law of Karma Yuga

Like Ezekial's "wheels a' turning within wheels," such events humble us with the realization that we are often but "small cogs" in a universal Karmic clock. Study the illustration (p. 53) well!

Notice that every cog meshes with another wheel, turning an outer wheel, which in turn rotates another set of three wheels turning another outer wheel, and thus projecting into the future.

Nothing can occur in our lives at a physical, intellectual, or emotional level that does not have repercussions into the future by consequences turning the "wheel of fortune," thus setting our *fate* or apparent destiny ahead of us.

The more you study this diagram, the more fascinating it becomes. A whole new dimension of understanding emerges when you contemplate the idea that the present has resulted from the past and the future is being made now!

An even more fascinating perspective is evident when you consider that the future arises from the past and perhaps the future dips back into our present? In the words of the great German philosopher Nietzsche:

> Our Destiny Rules over us,
> even when we are not yet aware;
> it is the future that makes laws for our *today*.
>
> — *Human, All too Human* (1878)

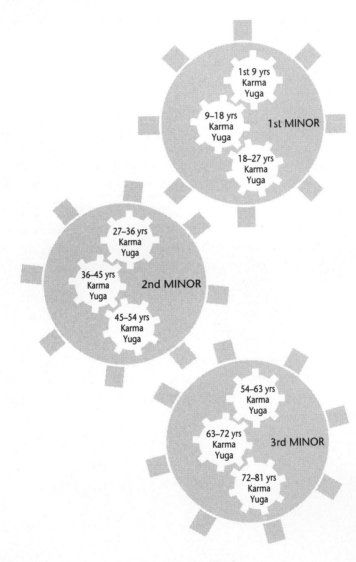

**The Karmic Clock**

Dr. Swami Gitananda often quoted the Hindu/
Buddhist axiom:

> Sow a thought, reap an action,
> Sow an action, reap a reaction,
> Sow a reaction, reap a habit,
> Sow a habit, reap a characteristic,
> Sow a characteristic, reap a DESTINY.

Hinduism teaches that life activity should be cen-
tered or directed appropriately in four distinct phases or
cycles. These are:

- *Bramacharya:* the educational and student phase
  of life, traditionally birth to twenty-five years of
  age; in Yantra it is twenty-seven years of age

- *Grahastha:* This is the productive, family, and
  professional period— the working time of life;
  in Yantra it lasts until fifty-four years of age

- *Vanaprastha:* Retirement from active life, leisure,
  and serious movement toward the interior life
  through meditation and worship until eighty-one
  years of life

- *Sannyasa:* Absolute renunciation of everything
  but God; may be taken at any time in life, but traditionally after eighty-one to the end of life

No matter how small a thought or action the great Wheel of Life is turned. Every movement of mind and body in infancy and childhood moves or influences the 9, 18, and 27 year Karma Yuga cycle; While the first Minor Dharma Yuga, the Brahmacharya Ashrama (educative period) is setting the stage for the Second Minor called the Grahastha Ashrama, from 28 to 54 years{Productive period) and the third Dharma Yuga, the Vanaprastha Ashram (Leisure Period from age 55 to 81). Every movement in time and space is effecting the spiritual life represented by the outer wheel.

— Swami Maharishi, Dr. Gitananda Giri

The Karma Yuga chart is the psychic flow equivalent diagram echoing Freud's dictum "Biology is destiny," and Anna Freud's statement "We are what we are told we are."

# How Subtle Is Karma?

Let us imagine that two men are standing on a street corner. One man has a hole in his pocket and out of that hole slips a ten-dollar bill, which falls down upon the pavement. The other man, standing beside him, notices that the ten-dollar bill has slipped out of that person's pocket and he puts his foot over it, thus deliberately concealing it.

When the other man moves off, the second man picks up the ten-dollar bill and pockets it. We would agree that the intent, that is the attitude, the emotional posture behind that action, was outright thievery, and therefore we say, "OK, that is going to result in Karma."

The Agami Karma that will swipe the thief sometime later in his life is a consequence of the willful desire to steal. This example seems fairly clear cut. Remember, we are not in a circumstance where he might have been starving to death—we are just looking at the emotional intent.

What are we trying to understand? We are trying to understand the attitude, not the action itself. Two people can commit exactly the same act, but it is the attitude behind it that determines the Karma.

Consider this proposition. On the other street corner two more men also stand. One man has a hole in his pocket and a ten-dollar bill slips out of his pocket, unbeknown to him. Now the man who has lost the ten-dollar bill looks down and sees the money on the ground. He looks at the other person and assumes that it is the other man's ten-dollar bill, so he slips his foot over it and when the other person has gone, he steals it, not knowing that he has stolen from himself.

This is not exactly the same action, so will he accrue Karma? Yes, the Agami Karma! He has stolen from himself and one day when he least needs it, least expects it, the Agami Karma will start.

Both the above examples will accrue Agami Karma because the attitude was the same in both cases. Both men were outright thieves, and although one man stole from himself, he still suffers the Karma.

At this point we need to remind ourselves that Karma operates in the non-physical realms at a very subtle level. Robert Svoboda, the foremost Western expert on Ayurveda, has written about Karma in his book *Ayurveda: Life, Health and Longevity* (Penguin Books U.K., 1992):

> The law of Karma extends this physical law
> to the non-physical realms of existence: what-
> ever action of any sort, even mental, a being
> performs in the world will be returned in
> kind. Jesus said it in this way: "Do unto
> others as you would have them do unto you"
> for "as you sow, so shall you reap."

These differences are very, very subtle. It is the attitude, the emotional stance, and the feeling posture that we approach and act with that determines and brings into fruition Agami Karma.

Perhaps Shakespeare was alluding to *attitude* when he said:

> Though FORTUNE'S malice overthrow my
> state, my MIND exceeds the compass of her
> WHEEL.
>
> — *Henry VI*, iv, 3

Interestingly enough, this principle of attitude is enshrined in the Westminster legal system as *intent*. The *intent* to commit a crime is as punishable as the act of committing an offense. An overseas visitor who believed that toothpaste was illegal in Australia, and therefore conspired to make a fortune by smuggling it into the country in the hollow heels of his shoes, if caught at customs would go to trial. The fact that toothpaste is perfectly legal in Australia would make no difference—this individual would be punished for intent to commit a crime!

When we deal with the subject of Karma it will not hurt us to remember a few things we can learn from our learned legal friends, including "ignorance of the law is no excuse."

# The Web of Karma

We often make premature judgments in placing "value judgments" on other people's activities; the truth of the matter is that the web of Karmic interactions that we all, knowingly or unknowingly, conspire to weave with each other is often beyond our comprehension.

Consider the following story and after reading this, rate the individuals in the story on a Karmic and Dharmic scale from most culpable to least blameworthy, and most responsible to least responsible.

# Alligator River

Once upon a time, a pair of star-crossed lovers lived on opposite sides of a large river filled with ferocious and hungry alligators.

Young Daphne dwelt on one side of the river and her childhood sweetheart, now her fiancé, Periwinkle, lived in a large mansion on the other bank of Alligator River.

One night a dreadful typhoon struck and the river-banks overflowed, washing away the bridge.

About midnight Daphne received a desperate phone call from Periwinkle; "Darling, come and save me—a beam from the roof has fallen on me and I am bleeding to death."

The distraught Daphne ran straight out into the rain, hail, and lightning, desperately trying to find a way across the alligator-infested river. She quickly discovered the bridge was washed out and remembered that upstream lived a boatman who often ferried people across Alligator River. His name was Sinbad.

Absolutely soaked, Daphne arrived exhausted at Sinbad's front door and vigorously banged on it with the strength of the terrified.

Sinbad, who was quite annoyed at being awakened, answered the door and softened immediately upon seeing the lovely Daphne. He had often looked at her with lascivious eyes.

Daphne poured out the story of how Periwinkle was trapped under a beam in his house, that the bridge was washed out, and she needed Sinbad to take her across in his boat.

Sinbad realized opportunity had just knocked and he forthwith made a very straightforward proposition to Daphne—in fact that is exactly what he made—a proposition. If Daphne went to bed with him then, after an hour, he would take her across Alligator River.

Daphne was horrified and ran, weeping hysterically, back out into the rain, lightning, and hail. Totally distraught, she ran down the side of the riverbank and bumped straight into Smith, her next-door neighbor.

Sobbing in his arms, she told him the whole dreadful story: how Periwinkle was trapped and bleeding to death under a wall in his house, the bridge was destroyed by the storm, the alligators were thrashing around on the overflowing river bank and she nearly lost a leg and an arm, and how she had asked Sinbad to get her across the river in his boat, and that he had demanded she sleep with him as payment—and in advance!

When Smith had heard the whole story and Daphne had asked him for help, he released her from his arms and said: "Daphne, in life we all have our crosses to bear and I cannot get involved—in fact it is way past my bedtime and nearly 2:00 A.M., so I will just have to leave you. Good night," and Smith left her standing stunned in the downpour.

Reality, in fact the kind that can lead to self-actualization and self-realization, struck Daphne, and she ran back in the pouring rain to Sinbad's house.

Sinbad drew a hot bath for her and dried her drenched clothing in front of the fireplace, and she made Sinbad a happy man—very happy indeed! Sinbad, true to his word, ferried her across Alligator River and deposited her on the bank near Periwinkle's mansion.

She threw open the front door at Periwinkle's and rushed in to find him sipping a hot rum in front of his roaring fireplace, ensconced in his favorite armchair.

They stared at each other with mutual amazement.

"Daphne, my dear, what are you doing here at 4:00 A.M. in the morning? If you don't mind me saying so, you look dreadful—thoroughly disheveled—you are not usually careless about your grooming. Would you mind standing on the doormat? I don't like the polished floorboards being dripped on! Anywise, I got myself out from under the beam and stanched the hemorrhage. I have consistently tried to ring you to tell you everything is fine, but you were not answering all night—a bit inconsiderate of you. Have you been out this evening?"

Daphne promptly burst into tears and told him the horrible story: how the bridge was washed out and she was desperate to help him and Sinbad would not ferry her across the river unless she slept with him, and how her neighbor Smith was unwilling to help and how in the end she went back to Sinbad's and slept with him.

"You what?" roared Periwinkle. "You are my fiancée—you are not supposed to be whoring around with a fishmonger! Get out! I never want to see you again!" and he promptly threw her down the front steps and back into the torrential rain, hail, and lightning.

Daphne ran sobbing down the street and nearly knocked over a distant acquaintance of Periwinkle's named "Spike." Spike's main interest in life was bodybuilding and weightlifting.

Daphne broke down and revealed the total horror of the evening: how the bridge was washed out and she was desperate to help Periwinkle; how Sinbad would not ferry her across the river unless she slept with him;

how her neighbor Smith was unwilling to help; and how in the end she went back to Sinbad's and slept with him . . . and how Periwinkle had broken the engagement and thrown her out into the street when he discovered what she had done.

Spike grabbed Daphne by the arm and dragged her back to Periwinkle's house. Spike pounded on the front door, and when the surprised Periwinkle opened the door, Spike broke Periwinkle's jaw with a superb right-cross hook and shouted at him: "Let that teach you to have more consideration and treat ladies properly!"

The end.

# What Is Your Judgment?

Some genius in the 1970s invented this story to teach a "Values and Ethics" course, and although it might seem silly to you, it is really no more absurd than the real life dramas in the sleazy weekend tabloids or the slop on some of the talk shows.

With a group of friends, try to rate all the characters in the preceding story, from the most reprehensible to the most innocent, and explain or justify your reason for each choice. The best way to do this is to read them this story from the book and then hand out pieces of paper with the names of the five characters, in order of appearance, in the story: Daphne, Periwinkle, Sinbad, Smith, and Spike.

With a group participating in this exercise you will learn about the web of Karma we all build and the impossibility of judging a Cosmic law by human standards. You will learn more than you could by any other means.

Just as views change between countries, cultures, and families, so the Karma accrued in the same situation will be different according to countries, cultures, and families. For example, the Karma accrued by a strict Protestant or Muslim who placed an extremely high value on sexual fidelity would be quite different from the Karma of a sexually liberated woman.

Later in this book I will further illustrate the complexities of Karmic patterns with a twister of a story from the 1990s.

# Karma Processing Factory: Assembly Line Four

*Who was or is this person—your father?*
*What was your father's main comment*
*to you or his attitude to life?*

The psychologists say that we progenerate our psychopathologies from generation to generation!

This is a formal way of saying we perpetuate Karmic patterns learned from our parents and thus deepen the web. A very thought-provoking fact!

Comments from others:

Who was or is this person—your father?
*"He's nothing, emotional development about*
*three; the man who was never there. Mother*
*always tried to provoke a reaction from him. He*
*had no emotion, he used to beat me for crying*
*when I shouldn't. A ham radio fan who didn't*
*like being disturbed by us. He never finished what*
*he started, indifferent person, a nonentity who*
*lives with his defacto [wife] who looks like a*
*shop-soiled, retired streetwalker."*

— Female, eighteen, university student

Who was or is this person—your father?
*"Gray-haired, talks at you, looks away, lot of*
*anger, cranky, loud voice, talks about himself and*
*his hard life, boring, always saying how much*

*money he could have made; he was stupid with money, gambled, held menial jobs and handed his pay packet to my mother."*

— Male, twenty-five, taxi driver

What was your father's main comment to you or his attitude to life? *"Take up a trade—I am disgusted with you: A trade is your only chance."*

— Male, twenty-five, taxi driver

What was your father's main comment to you or his attitude to life? *"'You're a no-hoper!' He put my hand on a hot stove once to punish me when I was eight. A friendship is like porridge, if it is too thick it burns!"*

— Male, twenty-eight, divorced,
unemployed for most of life,
and heavily involved in the drug scene

# Assembly Line Four: Process One

*Who was or is this person—your father?*

# Assembly Line Four: Process Two

*What was your father's main comment
to you or his attitude to life?*

## Meditation Focus

Tis the sunset of life gives me mystical lore,
and coming events cast their shadows before.

— Thomas Campbell, 1777–1844
*Lochiel's Warning*

# 5
# PRARABDHA KARMA

 ## Sprouted Karma

The third type of Karma is known as *Prarabdha Karma*. Prarabdha Karma is Karma that has already sprouted and nothing can stop it. It is consequences that are absolutely one hundred percent unavoidable. No one can stop Prarabdha Karma!

It is Prarabdha Karma when the seed is sprouted and the consequences are already clearly and irrevocably manifest. Prarabdha Karma may be described as *Kinetic Karma*, i.e., in full motion.

SaBija Karma is stored before and during birth, and is so latent it could almost be called *Static Karma*.

*The seeds collected and stored in the past that have actually begun to grow; i.e., the Karma bearing fruit in the shape of actual events.*

—Heinrich Zimmer,
*Philosophies of India*

With Agami Karma, the seeds have been planted in the soil of this lifetime and are ready to shoot forth at the slightest irrigation stimulus—but sprouted by what? Sprouted by emotion! Agami Karma is *latent Karma* or *sleeping Karma,* but sleeping lightly!

## Redemption of the Sandals

When I was a young man in India, this is a story I often heard, with variations, about Gandhi. It is a fine example of positive Agami Karma that quickly transforms into positive Prarabdha Karma.

On his return to India after one of his international trips advocating independence for India, Gandhi was traveling to Delhi. As he stepped onto the train, one of his sandals slipped off and fell to the ground below. Immediately, just as the train started to move off, he removed the other one and threw it down.

"Why did you do that, Babajii?" asked one of his companions.

"The beggar who finds one, shall now benefit from two." Gandhi replied. They continued on their journey.

Twelve months later Gandhi visited a town for celebrations to the Goddess Lakshmi. It was crowded and he had, without meaning to, become separated from his companions. As he looked about for his party, he heard a voice shouting abuse behind him, "You are destroying our beloved Bharat!" Before Gandhi could turn around, he felt himself knocked to the ground and kicked in the side.

"Leave him alone!"

Gandhi heard a shuffling beside him and as he opened his eyes he saw a familiar sight, the sandals that he had left on the train line. Strong hands reached down to him and gently lifted him up.

"Take no notice of that ruffian, Babajii, he's a fool and up to no good. I was like that until a year ago."

"What happened to change you?" Gandhi asked, and he brushed the dust off his clothes as the story unfolded.

"I had nothing and was too full of resentment to do anything about it. However my friend wanted me to accompany him to a celebration."

"This is your opportunity to improve yourself," my friend said. "Join in the praise for Lakshmi, and the Goddess of prosperity will assist you."

"It's a long walk," I replied. "You at least have sandals to protect your feet. I have nothing and am not likely to get anything." Then just at that moment, as we were walking along the train line, I noticed a very fine pair of sandals indeed.

"You have no excuses now," my friend said, and laughed as I put them on.

"We walked there together and joined the celebration. There was much work to be done and with my new sandals, came a new attitude. Normally, I would begrudge anyone anything but I now helped everyone. In fact, one of the organizers of the celebration was so impressed that he gave me a job which I still have, to assist with all the celebrations here and in neighboring towns. Now I am a respected person in the community."

Gandhi looked into the man's eyes and said softly, "Thank you."

# Karma Processing Factory: Assembly Line Five

## What do you admire and like about yourself?

"Psychotherapy: Yoga for the West," is how I described the Karma Processing in the introduction. The journey into the interior life begins with self-examination.

> What do you admire and like about yourself?
> *"I don't take my anger out on others and I don't consciously try to hurt others."*
>> — Female, twenty-five, social worker

> What do you admire and like about yourself?
> *"I am easy to get along with, and my consuming interest is in my own mind-body interactions."*
>> — Male, thirty, psychologist

Fill the next page with those qualities you like about yourself. Often this can be difficult to do.

# Assembly Line Five: Process One

*What do you admire and like about yourself?*

*Meditation Focus*

What lies behind us and what lies before us are
tiny matters, compared to what lies within us.

— William Maran

**6**

# THE KARMIC CYCLE

 **Basic Types of Karma**

In the last three chapters we have established the basic types of Karma. These are:

- *SaBija Karma:* accumulated before or during birth, and the seeds are waiting to be sprouted; they haven't sprouted yet but given the right stimulus and external environment they will suddenly come up

- *Agami Karma:* as soon as the right emotion is there to trigger, it will come up and bang you; you accumulated it in this life and you will collect the bulk of it in this life;

repercussions from Agami Karma that are not experienced become stored as SaBija in the next round

- **Prarabdha Karma:** Karma that you are already receiving; Prarabdha Karma may have its origins in either SaBija or Agami Karma

There are many ways of classifying Karma in different Hindu philosophical schools, and in this book I have approached the subject in the simplest form by enumerating just three divisions. Notwithstanding this, a fourth type of Karma is useful to consider.

# Dridha Karma: A Special Category

Having enjoyed learning from my friends Hart Defouw and Robert Svoboda, I could not do better than quote from their wonderful book *Light On Life: An Introduction to the Astrology of India* (Victoria: Penguin Books, 1996) in regard to Dridha Karma:

> Dridha Karmas give fixed results because they are so difficult to change that they are practically non-changeable. These Karmas, pleasurable or painful, are destined to be experienced because of the intensity of their causes. Most people have noticed that from time to time an experience simply "happens," despite all efforts to avoid its occurrence. (p. 29)

> Remember that this kind of karma may be
> pleasurable as well as painful; as we all know,
> those who seem the least deserving are often
> those who get ahead in life. (p. 30)

The Sanskrit word *Dridha* may be, or often is, translated as "firm" and an alternative translation is "sticky"—a reference to those people and situations in life that we seem unable to escape, or are fated to be involved with. Dridha Karma is a bit like walking barefoot on flypaper or wallpaper glue.

Some things have no apparent cause—when we understand Dridha Karma we can appreciate that existence is a mystery that we can perceive but dimly. Hart and Robert use the word "confluence" as indicating a likelihood of Dridha Karma as read in the Horoscope. I am going to approach the subject using the concepts of *synchronicity* and *serendipity*.

*Dridha Karma often explains many intense relationships that appear incongruous or unavoidable.*

Carl Jung defined *synchronicity* as "two causally unrelated but psychologically meaningful experiences occurring simultaneously." An example of this is when you are thinking about someone and they phone you. Is it a coincidence?

Serendipity, on the other hand, is an accidental discovery while looking for something else—a happy accident, or perhaps "chance favors the prepared mind."

Both synchronicity and serendipity seem to operate at times. Is this mere coincidence, or does it reveal a psychic coherence and cosmic harmony?

I first heard the following anecdote from Dr. Dos, a wonderful and very elderly Rosicrucian psychiatrist. This is a superb example of Dridha Karma—that twist of fate that binds two people together inescapably and inexplicably.

## The Doctor

In the 1900s, at a country party on an aristocratic estate, one of the visitors' children fell into a pool and was in danger of drowning. At this time it was very unusual for a British estate to have a swimming pool, but not so unusual for a child to be unable to swim.

The gardener's son plunged into the water and saved the child. Later the parents of the young aristocrat asked the gardener how they could ever repay his son, who was about the same age as their child.

"I have been blessed with two bright sons. The eldest gained a scholarship to a medical school and is a ship's doctor. Now my younger son would like to follow in his footsteps," related the gardener.

"If your son is accepted into medical school in London, send him to us and we will look after him," the father responded.

At thirteen, the gardener's youngest son went to London and stayed with his brother, while serving as a shipping clerk. At eighteen he won a scholarship to the University of London Medical School. Good to their word, the family of the child he had saved supported the gardener's son until he graduated. During his studies he developed a special interest in bacteriology.

Now a qualified doctor, he served as a captain in the Army Medical Corps in France, where he realized that the antiseptics used to treat the wounded were killing their white blood cells and making the infections worse.

After the war he began post-graduate work at St. Mary's Hospital in London, and in 1919 became a professor at the hospital.

He started research on Lysozyme, an enzyme contained in human tears, after realizing that Lysozyme possessed what we would now call bactericidal properties—it inhibited the growth of germs.

This man was a kind of genius who loved a sloppy lab that he could play in—his biographers report that he loved to do "bacteria" paintings of landscape by dabbing colorless fluids into patterns on culture dish jelly. Later the different bacteria contained in the fluids would grow to manifest myriad colors and shapes.

In 1928 he discovered a growth in a petri dish that he was about to discard. This growth formed an impenetrable ring to bacteria—the growth was penicillin.

Our professor considered penicillin and its potential applications, but nothing of practical clinical value emerged until he was joined in the late 1930s by Australian doctor Howard Florey.

By 1940 he had isolated the penicillin and was ready to start testing on humans when a government official arrived at his laboratory with an urgent request. At this time pneumonia was the number-one killer in the world and had been so for many hundreds of years.

"A very important politician is dying of pneumonia. We believe he is the only person capable of getting us through the dangerous years ahead. It is vital to the safety of Britain that this man live and the government requests that you use your discovery to save this man," he was told.

The professor left immediately with the official for the hospital. As the professor approached the bed of the dying man, he recognized him as the aristocrat's son he had saved from drowning years earlier. The two gazed at one another with shock and pleasure.

Dr. Alexander Fleming injected with penicillin Winston Churchill, M.P., and once again saved his life. We all know the result.

Both men were later in life given knighthoods for their individual contributions to England. "Never has one man owed another man so much—twice over!" said Sir Winston Churchill about his friend Sir Alexander Fleming.

> It is a mistake to look too far ahead. Only one link of the chain of destiny can be handled at a time.
>
> — Sir Winston Churchill
> *Speech to House of Commons,* February 27, 1945

# Frying the Seeds of Karma

There is an interesting thing to consider. In the classical teachings it is said that he who is *Jivan Mukta* (Mukta means "free," Jivan means "life"), who is "free in life," can eliminate SaBija and Agami Karma by virtue of certain Kriyas and through the grace of self-realization— just as a seed that is fried can no longer sprout.

One of the basic teachings in Yoga is that if you want to work off your SaBija Karma and your Agami Karma, you can do so through *Karma Yoga.*

*Karma Yoga: The path of Yoga seeking realization through detachment from the fruits of all action and dedicating all activity to Ishvara (anthropomorphic aspect of God), or—in a more Western mode of expression—as exemplified by Ralph Waldo Emerson's dictum (1844), "The reward of a thing well done is to have done it!" The Karma Yogi seeks conscious, aware action. See the need, do the deed!*
— A Chakra & Kundalini Workbook

Karma Yoga is the intention to work without regard to the fruits of your work. You cultivate the attitude of renouncing or detaching from the fruits of your action. You can try by sheer work, by the mental and physical  perspiration of your being, to fry the seeds of SaBija Karma and Agami Karma, but even the realized, even those who are Jivan Mukta, cannot avoid Parabdhra Karma.

The only thing that can be done with Parabdhra Karma is to adopt an attitude of indifference and simply accept it with equanimity. Any emotional reaction compounds the cycle, building more Agami Karma, which later will mature as Parabdhra Karma.

Shankacharya gives this analogy. He says that if in a state of unenlightenment (or sleep) a hunter pursues a tiger in the jungle, and through the bushes sees the tiger and pulls the arrow back and releases it, when suddenly the bushes part and he perceives that it is not a tiger but a cow—it is too late!

Do you know that for Hindus the cow is sacred? To kill a cow is an absolute anathema, and there is nothing that can be done. Even though the enlightenment has come and the correct perspective on reality has appeared, it is utterly, absolutely too late and you must suffer the consequences of that act. Even enlightenment will not save you.

What is sometimes termed, in the West, *self-realization"* or *self-actualization* may sterilize most of the SaBija Karma and Agami Karma—cultivating *detachment* may ameliorate even Parabdhra Karma.

# Karma Processing Factory: Assembly Line Six

## *What do you dislike about yourself?*

Comments from others:

> What do you dislike about yourself? *"My physical appearance—I feel awkward and ugly"*
>
> — Male, twenty-eight, industrial cleaner

> What do you dislike about yourself? *"The fact that I am afraid all the time of endless things, getting sick, getting out of control, losing my sanity, being raped, physical violence, being robbed"*
>
> — Female, twenty-seven, single, living on psychiatric pension

Make a list of what you dislike about yourself. Then, using the following steps, set about changing those things you don't like. Setting realistic goals and time frames are important. To achieve changes:

1. Number your list of actions in the sequence from easiest to most difficult or from the most important to least important, or if you prefer, a combination of both.

2. Can the first item be tackled in one effort or does it need to be broken up into smaller steps?

3. Write the first item or step on a sheet of paper in large bold letters and include the amount of time you will allow yourself to achieve it. Make several copies to put up around your home, such as in your bedroom; when you first arise in the morning and before you go to sleep, think about:

   • What have I done so far toward this goal?

   • Has it been effective?

   • What else can I do?

4. Note the item and the results in your diary each day for the allotted period.

5. At the end of the period, review your progress and decide if you will progress to the next item or step; obviously if you achieve the desired result earlier, then progress immediately.

Further assistance can be found in chapter 7, "Shaping the Future," of my book *Magical Tattwas* (St. Paul: Llewellyn, 1996).

# Assembly Line Six: Process One

*What do you dislike about yourself?*

# Assembly Line 6: Process Two

*What actions will you take to change?*

*Meditation Focus*

Intelligence is quickness in seeing things as they are. (Clairvoyance?)

— George Santayana

# 7
# KARMIC WEB

 ## Attitude to Karma

There is no way, no Kriya, no Shakti that will absolve us from the Karma for certain actions in our lives. However Bhakti Yoga, Karma Yoga, and certain Shakti Kriyas have the capacity to fry the seeds of SaBija and Agami Karma.

Let us go back to a man hunting a tiger and look again at the idea that it is the attitude or the emotional stance that waters the Karma. I will approach the problem with two different analogies.

First of all, imagine that we have a glass that holds 500 milliliters of liquid. I fill the glass to the middle mark with the best French champagne, so there we have a glass with a quantity of the best champagne.

What statement would we make about that glass and the liquid in it? Those of us who are in a jolly mood might say, "Wow, it's half-full of champagne; superb." Those of us who are in a more negative mood may say, "Oh, that glass is half-empty of champagne." To the optimist it is half-full, to the pessimist it is half-empty.

In reality, and you can use this as a metaphor for self-actualization, the philosophically oriented correct statement about that glass is, "the glass contains 250 milliliters of French champagne." That is the fact, the reality statement. Now we can approach this fact from two different emotional orientations—either half-empty or half-full. Consequently too, when we drink it we will absorb the Karma according to our emotional perception of the situation.

Either we will experience joy at 250 milliliters of expensive French champagne or we will experience regret that *only* 250 milliliters of champagne is available.

Now we will consider another man hunting a tiger who releases his arrow and to his disappointment discovers it is not a tiger in which his arrow is buried.

## The Lovers

A young man and his lover are out in the forest. Suddenly a tiger leaps out, grabs the young woman, kills her, and runs off. The man is beside himself with grief and he determines, since he is an archer of some fame, that he will pursue that tiger to the end of his days, until he finds it and kills it.

So he spends day after day after day searching in the forest. One day he looks through the bushes, perceives the tiger, pulls back the arrow, thinking of that tiger having killed his lover and he releases the arrow. At that moment he discovers that he has shot the arrow into a rock. The wooden arrow with a steel tip on it has driven deep into the rock—six inches into solid rock!

Although he has failed to kill the tiger, his consequent reputation is stunning. He becomes known as the man who can send a wooden arrow with a steel tip six inches into solid rock. No one else can do that. For the next ten years, until he dies, he keeps trying to shoot arrows into rock and they keep bouncing off and breaking. He can never do it again!

Do you know what did it? In Yoga we call it emotional intent—will power. He had so much pent-up "Shakti" or energy in him, thinking it was the tiger, that he transmitted enough psychic force with the projectile to penetrate the rock. Never again could he bring up that amount of psychic force.

This story is a fable about the karma in your life and in my life. What is the intensity of rage, love, hatred, compassion, determination, passion, and every other aspect of emotion that is the human heritage on the journey to *humanness* we are undertaking? We may begin to perceive that our whole existence is a predictable karmic fabric determined by the *quantity* and *quality* of feelings we cultivate. *As a man soweth so shall he reapeth.*

# Weaving Our Karma

Now if we look at these three types of Karma, we can ask ourselves the question: "What to do?" We can also ask ourselves another question: "Just how subtle is this?"

It is very subtle, because I am suggesting that all of us are caught in a web that has no weaver except ourselves. We weave our own web with Karma—our life is made up of Karma: an endless cycle of *action* and *reaction*. Life is a delicate, precarious balance between *fate* and *free will*.

Is truth stranger than fiction? Consider the following little tale of contemporary horror, and as you read it contemplate where does free will end and fate begin?

# Karmic Quicksand

Paul, the husband of the young and beautiful Jacqueline, has been diagnosed with AIDS, contracted when a test tube broke while he was doing a blood analysis in the laboratory where he worked.

This laboratory specialized in AIDS research. After Paul was forced to leave due to ill health, the lab made a major breakthrough in AIDS treatment. This involved genetically engineering a new form of AIDS. Unfortunately this form easily mutates and quickly jumps the species boundary to infect a variety of animals. This new form of AIDS is not lethal for humans and while it still weakens the immune system, it destroys any of the lethal form of the AIDS virus present in the person. While humans can survive with this weakened form, animals in the wild cannot. It could destroy the world's wildlife population, leaving only pampered zoo animals to survive.

Jacqueline pleads with Paul's co-worker Roger to supply Paul with the drug. He agrees on the condition that she have sex with him, but after the event he reneges on his bargain. Jacqueline, frantic to obtain the drug, asks her sister Faith to reason with Roger. After a series of meetings, Faith and Roger fall in love, and Faith refuses to help Jacqueline force her lover to break the law.

In desperation, Jacqueline enlists the aid of the underworld figure, Mr. Big, who arranges to steal the drug for a fee.

Unknown to Paul, Jacqueline feeds him the drug in various foods and beverages. He stabilizes and regains a somewhat fragile but stable health, enabling him to lead a normal life. His doctors believe the AIDS virus has gone into remission, not realizing that a more benign one has replaced the original virus.

Mr. Big, impressed by Jacqueline's beauty, sees the opportunity to add Jacqueline to his stable of exclusive, high-class prostitutes and starts bribing her to create an environment where she will agree to his demands.

By this time Jacqueline realizes she is pregnant with Roger's baby.

Unable to cope with the pressure of the pregnancy, the demands of Mr. Big, or the worry that Paul now carries a virus that could destroy the animal kingdom, she confesses all. Paul is horrified over what she has done, demands that she have an abortion, and immediately contacts the Government Department for Wild-Life and Recreation, to advise them of the situation.

A government investigation is set up, resulting in Jacqueline's arrest and trial. However, with assistance from government legal aid and because of pressure from womens' rights groups (due to her pregnancy), her jail sentence is reduced to parole. By the time her baby is born, she has been forgotten by all. With no means of support, she is forced to give the infant up for adoption.

As a result of stress due to her guilt, the court case, losing her husband, being fired from her job, and having her baby taken from her, she has become mentally unstable, but adequate support for mental illness is not available. One day she waits for Paul outside his apartment and murders him as he is unlocking the door.

# Who Will Cast the First Stone?

Treating the above story as an exercise in value judgments and attempting to get a group to agree on rating each character's degree of culpability is an even more volatile group experience than considering "Alligator River."

I gave this exercise to a mixed group of Europeans and Indians in 1996, at Ananda Ashram in Pondicherry, India. The cultural differences in opinions about who was most reprehensible were amazing.

The Europeans were concerned more with external actions and moral judgments, while the Indians focused on what could be expected from the person according to their background, education, and status (caste) in society.

Without exception, the Indians paid no attention to "Mr. Big," as they considered he was of low caste, a mere *dacoit* or thug, and what could you expect from such a person?

The Indian consensus was that the heaviest Karma would accrue for Roger and Paul, as they were obviously educated Brahmins and had a much heavier Dharma or obligation to behave properly in the interests of society.

Jacqueline's sister Faith was thought to be a very heinous person because she betrayed the trust placed in her, while Jacqueline accrued minimal Karma because she acted from a pure plane of "Sattvic" love. Indian society still values an idealized concept of the feminine, and the strength of women to faithfully persevere in the face of obstacles is legendary.

Perhaps those who seek fame and fortune are always caught in a self-made Karmic net of fate and free will. We would all do well to contemplate Hippocrates' words 2500 years ago, in his opening paragraph of "Instructions to Physicians."

Art is long; Life is short;
Experience is dangerous;
Opportunity is fleeting,
And Judgment is difficult.

Nothing has changed in 2500 years. The fundamental hazards of contemporary life still manifest as a Karmic snake pit, or as I often observe, "existence is a Karmic minefield."

# Karma Processing Factory: Assembly Line Seven

*What was the best part of your favorite book, tale, or story as a child?*

Some comments from others:

> As a child, what was your favorite book, tale, or story, and what was the best part of it? *"Alice in Wonderland. I really liked it when she was eating magic mushrooms, growing big and small, when she walked down a long passage and opened the door at the end."*
>
> — Male, twenty-eight, unemployed for most of his life and heavily involved in the drug scene

> As a child, what was your favorite book, tale, or story, and what was the best part of it? *"Little Red Riding Hood and I can still remember when the wolf dressed up in granny's clothes and climbed into bed to surprise Red Riding Hood. I sometimes think I am a wolf in sheep's clothing."*
>
> — Male, twenty-two, single, bartender.

> What was your favorite book, tale, or story as a child and what was the best part of it? *"A story about a statue of a boy angel who came to life and had to hide his wings with the clothing he wore. Everyone thought he was a hunchback and deformed, and all the time he was really an angel. No one understood."*
>
> — Female, forty-eight, married, manager

# Assembly Line Seven: Process One

*What was the best part of your favorite book,
tale, or story as a child?*

# Assembly Line Seven: Process Two

*What do you think this reflects about you?*

*Meditation Focus*

The universe may be not only queerer than we think, but queerer than we can think.

— G. B. S. Haldane

# 8
# KARMA: GOOD AND BAD

 **Retribution and Karma**

Have you noticed the way I am talking to you? In the Western Judaic tradition, our minds are used to thinking in terms of Karma as something bad—we have this Judaic Christian attitude. Fortunately, I am half Hindu—my right hemisphere is Hindu.

We also unwittingly embrace the Judaic-Christian concept, an eye for an eye and a tooth for a tooth. Somehow, when we start dealing with the Western concept of Karma, we associate Karma with punishment or pain. Karma has nothing whatsoever to do with penalty, punishment, or pain—such concepts are relative and it is all in the eye of the perceiver.

This association of pain, punishment, and penalty seems a psycho-linguistic heritage of Europeans; all three words come from the same Latin root *poena,* and we forever are doomed to associate them with each other. This is quite childishly apparent in the American psyche, for instance, when the pain of poverty is often assumed to be a sign of punishment and penalty, while wealth is an obvious sign of God's blessings and favor.

There is actually no retribution involved in Karma. Karma is a Universal law of action and reaction—inevitable consequences—it works all ways and *always.* Justice is a human concept, variable from culture to culture. Karma, from the Eastern view, is not a human concept, but a transcultural fact that belongs to the larger inherent Cosmic order.

## Good versus Bad

Some of you must have pet birds at home that you just adore. They talk and they sing—for some people, birds are their major companions. If the cat next door breaks open the door of the cage and eats the bird, it is bad for the bird—it is good for the cat. It might be bad for you and the bird, but the cat is delighted—it's got a smile from ear to ear, a regular Cheshire cat!

So it is in the emotional area. There is no such thing as good or bad Karma—everything is relative. Karma has to do with our perception of a Universal law that acts within a cycle—some teachers suggest it is an endless round of birth after birth, life after life.

Have you ever considered, for example, why all of us haven't won the million-dollar lottery or the half million-dollar lottery? The answer is very simple. We don't deserve to win half a million dollars—if we did deserve it, we would have won the money.

From the other angle (and you may think this is crazy), what appears to be a good event can actually be a very bad event. What appears to be a bad event, conversely, can be a very good event. This is because things are not as they seem, and the function of Karma is to confront us with a growing edge. It is this Universal subtle web of Karma that allows us an opportunity to grow all of the time.

Do you know, for some people it would actually be bad to win a half-million-dollar lottery? It would be the worst thing that could happen to them. To win a half-million-dollar lottery destroys some people. It can destroy their incentive, destroy their family, destroy their children, destroy their will to work—it can be a form of Agami Karma with negative consequences.

Now, if you had nothing better to do it would be very interesting for you to go back nine years, locate nine people who have won a half-million dollars, and do a research story on what happened to each of those families over the nine years. That would be exceptionally interesting. For some people it would work out well, but I expect that for two-thirds of them it would have worked out rather badly. The reason most of us are not millionaires is that we don't deserve to be—it is not in our Karma, because being a millionaire has its own Karma.

# Karma for Growth

In life, each of us gets exactly what is necessary, at any moment in time, for us to grow. The Karma is our exact precise growing edge, so this idea of penalty and punishment that we associate automatically with Karma is not even a correct view in itself—it is a false value judgment.

Where each of us is, is exactly where each of us is, and it is exactly what we deserve, and exactly what we need. Everything that has happened in my life has happened because I deserved it. I live in this house at this moment because I deserve to live in this house. I also have a number of other things attached to me in this house that I may not feel too happy about, and I deserve those too.

# Do Accidents Exist?

When we consider examples of Karma, Dharma, and the intertwining of past, present, and future, it is very easy to become confused. We are also alternately talking about fate versus free will, and deterministic destiny versus self-determinism. You will often think I am making contradictory statements, but as you become familiar with this *right-brained* Eastern way of teaching, everything will fall into place.

Does "chance" or "accident" have a reality? The answer is "Yes" and "No." It depends on not only what you mean by reality, but also your understanding of "accident."

The Sanskrit equivalent of chance is *Lila,* a word that really translates better as "play," i.e. "Play of the Gods," and the suggestion is that we are toys of the Universe and our interpretation of many events cannot help but be "accident." Events happen that are not personally related to us, but in fact are all part of the design.

Perhaps I will just leave your unconscious to ferment upon this mystery by giving you the following wonderful quotation from the last century:

> How true it is that our destinies are decided
> by nothings and that a small imprudence,
> helped by some insignificant accident, as an
> acorn is fertilized by a drop of rain, may raise
> the trees on which perhaps we and others
> shall be crucified.
>
> — Henri Frederic Amiel,
> *Journal*, April 9, 1856

# Karma Processing Factory: Assembly Line Eight

### *What is your favorite flower?*
### *What is your favorite object?*

Comments from others:

What is your favorite flower? *"A dandelion: blow it and it scatters in all directions."*

> — Female, twenty-three, student, recovering from a nervous break(through)down

What is your favorite flower? *"A yellow-petaled four-leaf clover for luck and to match my fear!"*

> — Male, twenty-eight, industrial cleaner

What is your favorite object? *"A blank wall—anonymous."*

> — Female, twenty-three, student

What is your favorite object? *"A spear so I could be hurled out at others with impunity."*

> — Male, twenty-eight, industrial cleaner

# Assembly Line Eight: Process One

*What is your favorite flower?*
*Explain why, and what the qualities of the*
*flower are that attract you?*

Another way of expressing this is:

*If you were a flower, which one*
*would you be, and why?*

## Assembly Line Eight: Process Two

*What is your favorite object?*
*Explain why, and what the qualities of the*
*object are that attract you?*

Another way of expressing this is:

*If you were an object, which one*
*would you be, and why?*

## Meditation Focus

There is no cure for birth and death, save to enjoy the interval.

— George Santayana

# 9
# ESCAPING KARMA

 ## What We Deserve

There are at least two laws, Karma and Dharma, and there is no way of avoiding these universal injunctions—you can only understand them and work within their parameters.

Let me tell you something more. By the time I was about fourteen, I wanted four things: I wanted to be a writer, I wanted to be an international lecturer, and I wanted to be a physician. Guess what—I got all three things. But I said there was a fourth thing I wanted; *I didn't want any responsibility.*

Guess what? I got responsibilities all my life, from which I could not run away, and it left me screaming down the corridors of my mind. I even went to India thinking I could avoid responsibility. I did not want this family, this productive thing, this middle-class existence, I did not want any of this, and especially I did not want to be responsible for anybody. Did I get my Karma! I deserved it thoroughly and I am still getting it.

What we get is exactly and absolutely suitable for our own personal growth. We need to constantly be reminded that Karma is exceptionally subtle, that it is a personal growth tool. In *Galatians*, Paul says: "Be Yea not deceived, God will not be mocked, for as a man soweth, so shall he reapeth."

*It is rumored that Mahatma Gandhi stated: "After devising Karma, God was able to retire!"*

We have much more control over our lives in terms of individual responsibility than we care to acknowledge.

## What Is God?

In this particular esoteric school, along with a number of other esoteric schools, we have a definite idea about God. God is a *process*—like Karma—not a being, not a person, not something you can touch. God is a *process*.

---

That process in Hinduism we call Brahma, Vishnu, and Shiva: G(eneration), O(rder), and D(isintegration). As we often joke in our classes, the Universe is just one big compost heap and GOD is manure!

So it says, "Be ye not deceived, God will not be mocked." There is no escape from the process—the process is one of birth, life, death: Generation, Order, Disintegration. You can't mock that and there is no escape from it. "As a man soweth, so shall he reapeth." And if you are like me, then sometimes when you reap what you have sown, you will cry.

The Yiddish language has an expression: *hutzpah*. Do you know what hutzpah is? I can demonstrate hutzpah when I am weeping unrealistically about my Karma, the inevitable consequences of my actions. Have you ever complained and wept about what is happening to you? "This is terrible!" "Why me?"

What the Jews call hutzpah is the classic story of the boy who murders his mother and father, and then pleads before the judge for clemency and mercy on the grounds that he is an orphan. Now, isn't that you and I? I know I have done that many times. I have set things up, organized things, and then the consequences fall— why me, why me? And this is what we tend to do with our lives.

We have an unbelievable knack for misunderstanding each other, even when Dridha Karma has attracted us to another person with a similar karmic pattern.

# Occupational Health Hazards

The policeman married. Four years and three children later, his wife realized how overworked, underpaid, and alienated she was—enslaved by little people who alternately screamed "Help!" or abused her. Whatever she did, someone was displeased.

"Occupationally, we have a lot in common," she remarked wearily to her husband one day.

He looked at her vacantly, uncomprehending.

# Is Our Environment Responsible?

We also have a propensity to imagine that the circumstances and the time we live in are uniquely difficult or special, and consequently our personal happiness is outside our control.

We need to be reminded of Charles Dickens' opening paragraph to his famous *A Tale of Two Cities*, published in 1859:

> It was the best of times, it was the worst of
> times, it was the age of wisdom, it was the age
> of foolishness, it was the epoch of belief, it
> was the epoch of incredulity, it was the
> season of Light, it was the season of Darkness,
> it was the spring of hope, it was the winter of
> despair, we had everything before us, we had
> nothing before us, we were all going direct to
> Heaven, we were all going direct the other
> way—in short, the period was so far like the

present period, that some of its noisiest
authorities insisted on its being received, for
good or for evil in the superlative degree of
comparison only.

# Karma Processing Factory: Assembly Line Nine

*What is your favorite animal?*
*Describe why it is your favorite, and the*
*qualities of the animal that attract you?*

Comments from others:

> What is your favorite animal? *"Panthers. They are long, sleek, black and have strength, physical fitness, and grace."*
>
> — Male, twenty-eight, industrial cleaner

> What is your favorite animal? *"A whale, alone, free and it can return to the pack."*
>
> — Female, twenty-three, student

# Assembly Line Nine: Process One

*What is your favorite animal?*
*Explain why, and describe the qualities*
*of the animal that attract you.*

Another way of expressing this is:

*If you were an animal, which one*
*would you be and why?*

## Meditation Focus

I don't know what your destiny will be, but one thing I know: the only ones among you who will be really happy are those who have sought and found how to serve.

— Albert Schweitzer, 1875–1965

# 10
# KARMA AND THE BHAGAVAD GITA

 ## The Clan Feud

The final, most primal, most basic analogy I can give you is to go back in mythological time, fifty thousand years ago (in historical linear time by our Western ideas, we would say 1000–500 B.C.), to that great Hindu epic, the *Mahabharatha*.

The *Mahabharatha* has a section in it which most of you are probably familiar with, that great book called the *Bhagavad Gita* (The Song of God). The *Bhagavad Gita* is a story about the Indian knighthood, about a feud or vendetta between two great clans, the Pandus and the Karus, and their willingness to battle for possession of a great kingdom.

We are told that thousands upon thousands of years ago, in mythological time, these two great interrelated clans were drawn up on a battlefield with a lot of troops and chariots on each side. A hundred thousand troops and chariots on each side, the two mightiest armies the world had ever seen, drawn up ready to confront each other to settle a feud, a vendetta that had been going on for many years.

The leader of the Pandus was Arjuna, and Arjuna had as his personal charioteer and tutor, Krishna.

Arjuna drew his chariot up before the battlefield with his troops behind him. He looked at the men in the opposing army and saw many that he had grown up with. Some of them had been his own tutors, Bhimsa who had taught him archery, and others arraigned on the side of the Kurus.

He realized that soon these mighty armies would clash and he would kill the men he had grown up with, men who had been his own tutors. He threw down his weapons, his bow and arrows, and he despaired. Krishna came to him.

## How Do You Handle Karma?

I am going to mention a basic principle that I believe gives a key to all sacred writing. In esoteric philosophy it is a fundamental rule that any given statement is to be explained from a two-fold aspect; that is, as having an exoteric (outer) meaning, and an esoteric (inner) meaning.

The great religious texts are most commonly taken at the lowest common meaning and as dubious history for teaching the masses. Such an approach is fraught with pitfalls, as witnessed by the long legacy of dogmatism, intolerance, and the contemporary emergence of "Fundamentalism" so sadly and dangerously prominent in the Semetic triad of Judaism, Christianity, and Islam.

As Jonathan Swift commented: "We have enough religion to hate each other, but not enough to love one and another."

It follows that we must be careful about accepting a literal interpretation, or even historical, of any of the world's religious texts and should consequently always look beyond the obvious to the inner context.

The rule for ascertaining the correctness of an esoteric interpretation depends on one criteria: does the interpretation satisfactorily convey a message in the language of symbology that is beyond space, time, history, and science, and that is universally relevant for all people, regardless of religion, race, creed, gender, or dogma?

All the world religious texts converge in this *sacred space* and exhibit amazing correspondences. For example, Christ's New Testament statement, "I am the vine," is echoed by Krishna's words in the *Bhagavad-Gita* "Amongst all trees I am the true vine."

The entire *Gita* is a textbook on Karma Yoga. It is a textbook on how to handle Karma, how to conduct one's self in life. Let us examine the general theme of "the song of God," and search for an inner context, which would allow us to draw inferences of an allegorical nature having universal application.

The war chariot in which Arjuna and Krishna discourse is the physical body or *Deha*, that vehicle for expression of consciousness. The disease to which man is subject results from failure of consciousness (Arjuna) to heed and follow the directions of supraconsciousness (Krishna).

Arjuna is the self-conscious mind (*Ahamkara*) in its unawakened, unrealized state. As individuals, we are all in Arjuna's difficult position, on the battlefield of life with only our higher self (Charioteer) to steer and guide us.

Krishna is the Christ consciousness in each of us, the Guru Atman, a part of ourselves that actually *knows*— the supraconscious guidance latent within us all.

Arjuna's decision concerns the choice we must make during our journey from womb to tomb. Have we the courage to accept our Karmic and Dharmic obligation to fight, battle, struggle, and eventually conquer the lower self? This is the eternal battle raging within each of us.

The mind (Arjuna) must follow the urging of *Christ consciousness* (Krishna), and through the discipline of the five senses (Pandus) conquer and gain control of the emotions (Kurus) on the battlefield of life (Kurukshetra).

Krishna said to Arjuna: "Be yea not deceived, I am acting through you, I am in everyone, I am you and I am in your brothers, I am in the Kurus and the Pandus. This is a Cosmic plane and your Karma at the moment: your action that is required is that of a Kshetra or a warrior, and it is to kill with detachment, that is to fulfill the duty."

In that statement he gives one of the keys to handling our personal Karma. The key is renunciation from the fruits of the action—an attempt to cultivate total detachment. The entire Gita is Krishna's explanation to Arjuna of Karma Yoga and Bhakti Yoga and how a person can conduct himself in life.

The battlefield on which these two mighty armies are drawn up is called *Kurukshetra*. The opening passages of the *Gita* start with the blind King of the Kurus in his courtroom. Although the King of the Kurus is blind, literally he cannot see, he has a soothsayer, a seer, a clairvoyant in his court, and through that soothsayer's clairvoyant vision he is watching the two armies drawn up and he is waiting to hear the results of the battle.

# The Battlefield of Life

Do you know what that *Gita* is about? That *Gita* is every man's life, every woman's life, every person's life. It is your life and my life.

Arjuna is the part of ourselves emerging as ego, that part of ourselves that is attached to ourselves, the part that says I am about to be hurt, either emotionally or physically.

Krishna is the Atman, the part that knows that the whole thing is a Cosmic play.

Kurukshetra, the battlefield, is life itself, in which
you and I are involved whether we like it or not, for
there is no escape. Kurukshetra is the plane of our existence, upon which each one of us must live, struggle,
and die—your life and my life!

It is a game, it is a Cosmic game, and the only choice
you have is whether you are a good game player or a
bad game player. We are here on that battlefield of
life—like it or not.

Perhaps that was the injunction of the Old Testament writer when he said:

> Cast thy bread upon the water for thou shalt
> find it after many days.

> — *Ecclesiastes*, 2:1

The Pandus are the five senses. From those five senses we get impulses (whether they are from a past life or
this life), and we receive impression. It is our reaction to
the input that engenders emotions and thus determines
our Karma.

The Kurus are the emotions, and what manifests
Karma? The emotion or feeling is the water sprouting
Karma. Karma can be good or bad, depending on our
feeling about it, but it is through emotion, including
love, that we manifest certain types of Karma. It is
through hate (merely another variety of feeling) that we
manifest other types of Karma.

Thus the two armies symbolize the positive and negative forces in life; good and evil, white and black,

Shiva and Shakti, matter and energy, and all apparent opposites conceivable to the human mind.

The two armies arrayed and ready to clash represent precisely our position in life. We are constantly being torn between positive and negative feelings, between the desires and allure of our five senses and the emotional responses which their action awakens in our unconscious with resulting conscious reactions.

Arjuna holds back from fighting relatives on the side of the Kurus (his self-created negative emotions), and in life how many of us really wish to fight with and destroy the negative aspects of our own personalities? He hesitates to battle with his former archery teacher, for Arjuna, like us all, has learned through the self-same emotions that later turned against us or escaped our control.

The whole *Gita* is about the story of each person's life. The *Bhagavad Gita* is the story of each person's life and the spiritual possibilities therein. It is a parable of the struggle between the higher and the lower self; the David and Goliath locked within everyone.

Do you remember I said to you that it is the *attitude*, not the *action*, that determines the Karma? Two people can commit exactly the same action; one accrues this uncomfortable Karma, the other accrues no Karma. It all depends on the feeling invested.

*The supreme self is rooted in the knowledge of the self-controlled man whose mind is perfectly serene in the midst of pairs of opposites, such as cold and heat, joy and sorrow, honor  and ignominy*

— Kalyana Kalpataru,
*Gitta-Tattva Gorakhpur*

The King of the Kurus is blind. Do you know what he is blind with? Symbolically or metaphorically, he is blind with rage (it is rage that makes us blind). It is rage that particularly manifests Agami Karma and turns Agami Karma into Prarabdha Karma, sprouting it.

The King, Dhritarshtraa, is blind, and it is just such blindness produced by raging passion that makes emotion ruler of our lives, displacing Arjuna, the true King, who has as part of his inheritance Christ Consciousness (Krishna) or self-actualization.

Prarabdha Karma is Agami Karma that has sprouted— too late to stop it. It is through our senses, our positive or negative interpretation of the sense material that comes into us and our attachments, that we cause the Karma. Our reactions to these senses, depending on our individual natures, feed our Karma.

*As a light does not flicker in a windless place, such is stated to be the picture of the disciplined mind of the Yogi practicing meditation on the absolute.*

— Kalyana Kalpataru,
*Gitta-Tattva Gorakhpur*

The whole story of the *Gita* is a textbook of Karma Yoga. We are in a battlefield called "life." Each one of us is fighting for our sanity—this is what each of us, in our philosophical life, is primarily concerned with. The Gita is an allegory about the battle for our sanity and this is what life is about! When the Karma turns in a certain direction, we may feel we are literally going insane. When the Karma turns in another direction, we can grasp our sanity.

# Karma Processing Factory: Assembly Line Ten

## How do you expect to die and how old will you be?

How do you expect to die and how old do you think you will be? *"By painless suicide on the beach at age twenty-seven."* He didn't.

— Male, twenty-six, single, unemployed

How do you expect to die and how old do you think you will be? *"Shot for seducing women at age 109."*

— Male, thirty, psychologist

## What will it say on your gravestone?

What will it say on your gravestone?
*"He lived beneath the moon*
*He basked beneath the sun*
*He lived the life of going to do*
*And dies with nothing done."*

— Male, twenty-six, single, unemployed

What will it say on your gravestone?
*"He Tried!"*

— Male, thirty, psychologist

# Assembly Line Ten: Process One

*How do you expect to die?*
*How old do you think you will be?*

# Assembly Line Ten: Process Two

*What will it say on your gravestone?*

Write your own epitaph, your own eulogy, or obituary:

## Meditation Focus

Said the Eye one day, "I see beyond these valleys a mountain veiled with blue mist. Is it not beautiful?"

The Ear listened and, after listening intently awhile, said, "But where is any mountain? I do not hear it."

Then the Hand spoke and said, "I am trying in vain to feel," and the Nose said, "There is no mountain, I cannot smell it."

Then the Eye turned the other way, and they all began to talk together about the eye's strange delusion. And they said, "Something must be the matter with Eye."

— Kahlil Gibran
*The Eye*

# 11
# CYCLE OF REBIRTH

 ## Being Reborn

I will put together what we have established about this doctrine of Karma—it is a doctrine that we could have a lecture on every week for months and months, so you must understand that this has been very rapid.

I told you that within the doctrine of Samsara, or birth after birth, there is an esoteric teaching. What I pointed out is that you do not have to accept that as a proof that there is life after life. I would suggest to you, and I could show you although I have not the time now, that definitely the nine months of intrauterine life are of tremendous importance—that is when you get the bulk of your SaBija Karma. For you women who are pregnant, it is a time to meditate, to provide beneficial and positive influences to your nervous system, because what you are doing now will determine the SaBija Karma that your child is born with.

However, we are literally caught in a cycle of birth after birth—we are reborn, every year, every month, every day—a complete cycle has birth, life, and death. Every day we awake in the morning, and we have something we call consciousness for the duration of the day, and we die at night in sleep.

Every day of the month we are reborn again and none of us here are the same people we were yesterday or last month or last year or nine years ago or eighteen years ago. We are actually different people because as each day passes by, each month, each year, our experiences change. As our experiences change and through absorption and assimilation of those experiences, we change.

It is only an illusion—the *Maya* or memory gives us an illusion that we are the same people. Memory gives continuity to our lives, but in actual fact the people sitting here with me now are not the same people they were nine years ago or twelve years ago. Nor am I the same person. We are changing without realizing it, and it is only the continuity of memory which gives us a sense that we are still the same person; in actual fact we are not the same person at all.

# Manu Matsya—Big Fish Eat Little Fish

You remember I told you that we could make value judgments about Karma. We perceive certain events as uncomfortable, other events as comfortable, so we label them good or bad Karma. It is like the budgie, good Karma for the cat, bad Karma for the budgie. That would be our value judgment.

There are a number of small laws in Hindu philosophies that are nonetheless absolute. One of them is called *Manu Matsya*. *Manu* is "lawgiver," from which we get the cognate English word "mind," and *Matsya* means "fish". Manu Matsya means the cosmic rule that "big fish eat little fish"—that is a law of creation.

Manu Matsya is a Cosmic law, whether you are talking about galaxies absorbing smaller galaxies, or people conquering people, or tigers eating cows, or whatever—it is a fundamental fact of life. It is not pleasant; most of these laws we feel are unpleasant, and we don't want to know, but they are nonetheless true. Big fish eat little fish, so don't be surprised when you encounter this fact of existence. If you were a four-foot weakling and you picked on a six-foot monster and then got battered, is there anything surprising about that?

# Do You Deserve to Win the Lottery?

I also said that we cannot really judge, we cannot estimate. Most of us haven't won the lottery because frankly we don't deserve to win it. If we deserved to win it we would, but if we win it we might find out it is bad, not good!

This is a true story. Many years ago, the former head of a large organization in Australia and chairman of the board of directors, whose name we will not mention, Sir X, was about to retire—a millionaire in his own right. His office boy, for a going-away present, bought him the first Opera House lottery ticket. At that time one of the first Opera House lottery tickets that was coming up was for a purse of about a hundred thousand dollars. The office boy gave the lottery ticket to this millionaire and Knight of the Realm.

Three weeks later, the millionaire won. They say money makes money—that is another rule too. The Knight of the Realm did not so much as say thank you to his office boy, he just accepted the hundred thousand dollars. And we say, "Oh, isn't that terrible?" No, it is absolutely correct.

Suppose he had given the eighteen-year-old the hundred thousand dollars or a portion of it? That office boy would have learned nothing. If he had been given that hundred thousand dollars, he would probably be nowhere. That young man received such a shock at his superior's greed and thoughtlessness that he determined to become a millionaire in his own right. The clerk did just that and went on to become one of Australia's most outstanding philanthropists. He got exactly what he needed for his personal growth and evolution.

# Peace of Mind

So there is a lot to think about. We must not take Karma as an eye for an eye and a tooth for a tooth—not that literally. He who lives by the sword dies by the sword, but none of this is literal. The first manifestations of Karma may be loss of peace of mind, or conversely, gaining peace of mind. Karma is far too subtle for gross literal interpretations. The price we pay for crimes may simply be mental and emotional disharmony—that is what happens.

When we commit violent acts, to which we are attached—that is, to which we have an emotional stance—the Karma we get back is disruption of our own mind; it is very subtle. It may not manifest instantly; it creeps up later. This applies to communities, to nations, and to the world. When we sow physical violence we may not get physical violence back, but what we may get is loss of peace of mind and/or insecurity.

# Karma Is Not Confined to Time Frameworks

Time, as it manifests to human consciousness, is an illusion, or at best very variable. When we are mentally engaged, time passes quickly. When we are asleep, time vanishes. When we are bored, time drags.

When we meditate, time may expand so that we sense the "spaces between the seconds," and often they are filled with bliss or *Ananda*.

Karma functions independently of our perception of time and so we often make judgments that allow the wicked to go unpunished! A process that functions on a cosmic or macrocosmic plane cannot be understood with our limited consciousness. Indeed, even the concept of *punishment* is subjective and relative, as is *reward*.

Let me fertilize your unconscious by telling you an apocryphal story about Karma and murder.

# The Murderer's Tale

Many years ago a young man had with a partner commenced a career as a building contractor. The partner and the young man soon had a very severe disagreement, and the young man's response to this was to lure his partner deep into a wooded area on the pretext of looking at a proposed building site that needed to be cleared. The young man then murdered his partner with a bullet straight through the head, and left the body to rot.

Months later the corpse was discovered. The police had no evidence or proof of who did it, so the murder mystery was never solved.

Twenty-five years later, the now no-longer-young man was the owner of the most powerful contract building company in the state.

One day his demolition-explosives chief asked him to come along and inspect a site to be cleared. The two drove into a deeply wooded area that seemed uncannily familiar to the boss. They stopped, and with a slight shock the man realized they had not only returned to the forest where he had murdered his partner decades earlier, but they were standing at almost the very spot where it happened.

His chief "powder monkey" chattered away, and they agreed to do a test stump blast and establish the center where the work of clearing would commence when the crews moved in.

The charge was buried in the roots of a stump that had once been a large tree and the two men backed off, trailing cable to a safe distance. The explosives expert pushed the plunger down and the charge ignited, blowing the stump free of the earth.

When the smoke cleared the boss was sprawled out dead, shot straight through the center of the forehead. The police autopsy revealed a bullet buried in the brain, apparently sent flying from the tree destroyed in the blast. Ballistic forensics tests indicated the type of bullet had been out of production for over twenty years.

This tale has many ramifications and bears contemplation. I could not do better than summarize by again quoting Hart Defouw and Robert Svoboda in *Light On Life* (Victoria: Penguin Books, p. 25):

> Everything does not happen all at once in our world, thanks to the inherent limitations of time, space and causation. A tree and the seed from which it sprang cannot exist simultaneously; the former must develop from the latter. Events occur in our universe according to a sequence which is scheduled by the Law of Karma on the calendar known as time.

# Is Karma a Teaching about Blame?

Is Karma a teaching about blame? Absolutely not! Karma is not a disguised Judeo-Christian doctrine of sin, punishment, penalty, and pain. Karma is recognizing that even if we cannot understand clearly, there is a reason for everything and everything is for a reason. Karma allows living for a reason and a reason for living. Karma is not about human concepts of "justly right," but an acknowledgement that all is "just right" at a universal level.

# Are Natural Disasters Karmic?

Since once the doctrine of Karma is accepted accident is removed from a rational universe, the answer to this question is yes! To understand why this is so we need to be in a profoundly altered state of consciousness—I was always taught that I am unworthy to understand natural disasters until I can get down on my knees and explain to the ants why I am about to utterly destroy their nest in order to plow a field.

Farmers frequently burn their fields to produce a rich layer of ash-covered soil. Who is the cosmic farmer?

# Is Tragedy Punishment from Past Lives ?

Are children who are dying of cancer being punished from past lives? No! Life is a mystery and it is a Western idea to approach everything with the logical, left

hemisphere of the brain. Karma, as a Cosmic manifes-
tation, cannot be fully comprehended by human intel-
lect, but Karma can be perceived as making sense out of
non-sense.

I will suggest an approach to the problem of human
tragedy. Supposing such events as children dying of
cancer represented the only way we could ever learn
compassion and pity? It may well be that we are all taking turns in this Cosmic play, over aeons of time, to
ensure that sensitivity and empathy emerge in the race.

The Karmic function of tragedy is to teach us
compassion!

# Karma Processing factory: Assembly Line Eleven

*What would you really want to change about yourself if a genie popped out of a bottle and offered to do it for you?*

Comments from others:

> What would you really want to change about yourself if a genie popped out of a bottle? *"Go back to birth so I could replant myself and grow straight instead of the way I am emotionally stunted now."*
>
> — Male, twenty-four, single, taxi driver, in orphanage until age six

> What would you really want to change about yourself if a genie popped out of a bottle? *"The way I feel about my mind and my physical appearance."*
>
> — Male, twenty-eight, industrial cleaner

What realistic steps would you take to bring about this change if the genie refused?

1. Work out a plan that will bring about changes; if you cannot think what to do, discuss your ideas with a close friend or a medical professional; your plan could include enrolling in a course, or joining a club, or meditating each day.

2. Write your plan in your diary and include check-points—notes to remind yourself to review your progress.

3. Keep a record of your progress in your diary.

4. Also read *Magical Tattwas*, chapter 7 "Shaping."

# Assembly Line Eleven: Process One

*What would you really want to change about yourself if a genie popped out of a bottle and offered to do it for you?*

## Assembly Line Eleven: Process Two

*What realistic steps would you take to bring about this change if the genie refused?*

## Meditation Focus

We can easily forgive a child who is afraid of the dark; the real tragedy of life is when men are afraid of the light.

— Plato

# 12

# NINE-DAY KARMA CLEARING PROGRAM

 ## A Subtle Program

The Karma Shakti Kriya routine is the most powerful technique I know to burn off Karma. It is equivalent to a deep-frying of the seeds in your being that represent potential SaBija and Agami Karma. This technique, Karma Shakti Kriya, was designed by Maharishi Dr. Swami Gitananda Giri of Tamil Nadu, South India, and taught to me in 1958.

Karma Shakti Kriya is a nine-day program that is neither difficult nor easy. Only twice in my life have I completed it perfectly, and yet I can tell you it is neither easy nor hard—it is very subtle.

# Timing

When we say it is a nine-day-cycle program this is an optimum time frame, as those of you who understand Indian Numerology will realize. It is also optimum to start on the new moon when it is waxing (when it is growing). Start on the first day of the new moon. These are natural cosmic cycles that are to your advantage.

There are nine points in this program. Each one of them is to be practiced and performed each day so that within every day of twenty-four hours you have nine karmic disciplines to complete.

# The Preliminary Discipline

The preliminary discipline for commencing the nine-day routine is to ban all media input from your life for the entire nine days of the Karma Shakti Kriya.

- No television

- No radio

- No newspapers

*This is an absolute and inviolate rule—there are no exceptions!*

In the 1930s, Dr. H. Spencer Lewis, the first Imperator of the second cycle of the Rosicrucian Order (AMORC), wrote a wonderful book called *Mental Poisoning* (San Jose: AMORC Books, 1987). Dr. Lewis was concerned with teaching people how to defend themselves against negative influences.

I would suggest to you that the biggest single source of mental poisoning and constant anxiety-provoking agitation is through television and newspapers. We live in a society of information overload, and we are bombarded through the media by psychological toxins that equal or exceed any ecological toxins.

You do not need to *know what is going on.* Watching, reading, or listening to the news before going to bed or first thing upon arising immediately adds to your Karmic cycles of action and reaction.

Watching television before sleeping, or before breakfast, are two time periods in which you are naturally hyper-suggestible and very much in a weakened and irrational state. To expose yourself to such stimulus is the mental equivalent of taking a bath in sewage.

There is a theory that television will destroy civilization and that your brain is automatically placed in a zombified, hypnotic state just by looking at the "box." I seldom watch television, very seldom do I ever scan a newspaper, and I know other people who follow the "no television" rule.

Karl Marx said: "Religion is the opiate of the masses," and that was the nineteenth century he was talking about. In the twentieth century I would suggest that *television is the opiate of the masses!*

You might think that I am some kind of fanatic—a simple right-winger ranting about the evils of visual violence and pornography on the screen? Even if only

educational and Walt Disney-type programs were per-
mitted on television, I still would have serious reserva-
tions. The only positive use of television as a growth
tool that I am aware of—aside from educational docu-
mentaries— is the Oprah Winfrey show. When Winfrey
attained a sufficiently powerful position she turned her
show into a positive vehicle for self-transformation,
with material designed to assist everyone with actual-
ization and self-realization material. She is a wonderful
woman who has fulfilled her dream and should surely
be "Woman of the Year" on a *TIME* magazine cover.

I have not the slightest doubt that the media is a
highly efficient education machine. So far as I can
observe, the education we have gotten is that the meaning of life is acquiring and buying things, and instant
media certainly quickly spreads terrorist methodology.
The idea that you can get all the attention in the world
by taking hostages, blowing up buildings, and holding
a planeload of passengers for ransom by taking the pin
out of a grenade got around the globe in twenty-four
hours—maybe less!

To read a newspaper you have to be at least semi-
literate and utilize higher brain centers in the process—
lessons on television involve instant visual display, neat-
ly bypassing anything resembling critical evaluation.

The damage to children in inhibiting the learning of
simple social skills and the encouragement to adults to
abandon social interaction in favor of passive watching
is a twentieth-century epidemic directly attributable to
the spread of television.

I am not asking you to agree with me—I am simply telling you that a *media fast* is essential for the nine days of the Karma Shakti Kriya. You may be surprised at how your anxiety level drops.

I also promise that anything necessary for you to know about, someone will tell you. Humans, in days gone by, actually depended on talking to communicate—as unbelievable and quaint as that may seem!

As a final note, I have certainly watched television in my life—one of the discoveries I made, and had this verified by my students, is that if you meditate immediately after watching television, you often find images from the program cropping up in your meditation, and you have to process them before going deeper.

You've heard the expression *GIGO:* "Garbage In—Garbage Out." Exposing yourself to the media while doing the Karma Shakti Kriya means that the rate of mental garbage in will exceed the rate of mental garbage out.

# The Program

The first two injunctions in the Karma Shakti Kriya are absolutely pivotal to the entire program. I wonder if you have ever considered what is the biggest source of Karmic repercussions in anyone's life?

The biggest single source of unhappiness and Karmic debt occurs from what comes out of our mouths—and it is nearly impossible to get most people to understand that they often exist at a *diseased* level of being by not monitoring their speech.

Swami Dr. Gitananda was fond of saying:

Small minds talk about people,
Mediocre minds talk about things,
Evolving minds talk about ideals.

Some of the nastiest people I have ever met were
strict vegetarians and highly disciplined Hatha Yoga
practitioners who considered themselves great Yogis
and teachers, and yet failed to control their speech.

In 1973 I was in Bihar State, India for the Golden
Jubilee celebration of the Bihar School of Yoga. Ten
thousand people were present and I remember one of
the Hindu lecturers very wittily commenting that Yogis
suffered "I" problems—most certainly he was not refer-
ring to "Eye" diseases.

At the end of one long day, Paramhansa Swami
Satyananda, who was chairperson for the conference,
wearily announced that he had started out life studying
veterinary science and some days he still felt like an animal doctor.

The concept of control of speech is totally seminal to
the Karma Shakti Kriya, and perhaps I could best sum
up by quoting the reported words of another Master:

15:10  And he called the multitude, and said
unto them, hear and understand:

15:11  Not that which goeth into the mouth
defileth a man; but that which cometh out of
the mouth, this defileth a man.

— *Gospel of Matthew*

# ❧ 1 ❧
# NO COMMUNICATION OF DISSATISFACTION

Do not communicate dissatisfaction with what you are doing at any given moment. Not with your circumstance, your family, your finances, your relationships, your education, or any other aspect of what is confronting you as you work in daily life.

You think that is easy? Try it! Only twice in my life have I successfully completed the entire nine-day program. In fact I challenge you—if you think you have got your act together—I challenge you to do it!

If you are dissatisfied with your lot, this first discipline will allow you an opportunity to evaluate and change your circumstances as an alternative to endlessly complaining. You will come to understand the old adage: "when all is said and done—more is said than done!"

The tongue muscles are universally the most overused muscles in the body—probably because exercising them reflexively requires neither effort, intelligence, nor concentration.

*Santosha means contentment—
the practice of being contented.
How? By living in present time,
forgetting the past, leaving the
day-dreams of the future,
keeping the energies of the
mind/body complex for the
present moment.*

*— A Chakra & Kundalini Workbook*

# no CRITICISM

Do not openly criticize any person, object, or your job. "Impossible" is a big word for this task; "difficult" is a more reasonable word when embarking upon this discipline.

This is a type of *mouna,* or silence. If you have ever been in a Satyananda Yoga Ashram of the Bihar school, there is a practice called *antar mouna*, where you experience total silence.

Now can you imagine if you do not express dissatisfaction of anything and you do not criticize any person, object, or your job, you start to build up psychic pressure? This means that your SaBija Karma and Agami Karma start to come up, and you start to be aware of what is waiting there inside the subterranean caverns of your mind. If you don't express dissatisfaction, the pressure builds up, so then what you do is the next part—point three.

Despite this age of "yuppy" diets, I am much more concerned about what comes out of my mouth than what goes into it—and so should we all.

Remember the Indian practice of Tapas:

> . . . the practice of indifference to discomfort when no useful purpose is served by taking notice of that discomfort . . . . a cultivated attitude of nonchalance to extremes.
>
> — *A Chakra & Kundalini Workbook*

## 🌀 3 🌀
## OBSERVE THINKING AND ACTIONS

You learn to constantly watch the relationship
between the thinking process and action. Sometimes
Karma manifests in the outside world, but it begins in
the mind.

What happens is that you build up pressure because
you are not expressing dissatisfaction about your life,
and you are not criticizing others. Now everything is
magnified inside the head and you start to watch—you
start to see how such a thought leads to such and such
a feeling, and such a feeling leads to such and such an
action. Only you can stop yourself, and the only thing
you can ever really control is yourself.

This allows you to make your life as you think, or at
least to observe your emotions to find out what is really going on in there. So watch the relationship between the thinking process and the actions. That arises
directly out of points one and two; it is a consequence.
We all have our own little Karma Processing Factory
going on inside.

> This self-study means that the act of living
> is a continuous process of learning. Stop
> learning, and you begin to die in a very
> special way. Psychologists know that at least
> fifty percent of senility is psychological—loss

of interest in life, loss of willingness to learn by life's experience. In this context, Yoga is a form of re-education.

— *A Chakra & Kundalini Workbook*

# ARISE EARLIER

Arise one hour earlier in the morning and practice yoga or martial arts. Anything involving physical activity with the body will assist to change the normal bio-rhythm of your body and thus enhance your personal awareness.

In India we used to get up at 4:00 in the morning day after day, month after month. If you are in the habit of rising at 4:00 A.M. (Swami Gitananda called this "God's hour," or *Brahma Hourti*), then get up at 3:00 A.M. during the nine days of Karma Shakti Kriya.

The quality of meditation at this time is remarkable. A lucidity blended with relaxation permeates the whole mind-body complex in quite a unique way. When I was young, my early experiences in both Northeast and South India were vivid when meditating before sunrise.

I must confess that I am not an early morning person in the West, and I absolutely abhor getting up early now that I am older, but those youthful experiences in India have never left me.

When you meditate before sunrise, Swami Gitananda taught that you get a wave of beneficial energy passing through the atmosphere as Usha, the Goddess of the Dawn sweeps over the horizon, with Surya, the sun, distantly trailing in her skirts. In fact, this is quite true in the sense that there is a special change in the ionic concentration of the atmosphere, and the whole electromagnetic balance of the stratosphere changes just before dawn.

Swamijii always likened meditating at this time to being inside a psychic balloon (the psychic bodies) or a "fish tank" where your thoughts were so slowed down it became easy to observe and control them.

# ❦ 5 ❦
## ONE MAJOR MEAL

Eat one major meal a day only, no meat, fish, or fowl—only fruits and vegetables—and drink a lot of pure water. This may produce some hypoglycemia, which will help to stir up all kinds of emotional reactions.

As these feelings emerge, you are not allowed to criticize or express dissatisfaction and consequently you really get a chance to discover (or uncover) the deeper aspects of yourself.

This is not a discipline about diet, nor even a physical discipline. It is a discipline about our emotional lives and a method of breaking out of ingrained patterns.

To remind you that this is not a dietary injunction, here is another little known statement of Christ:

> *15:17* Do not ye understand, that
> whatsoever entereth in at the mouth
> goeth into the belly, and is cast out into
> the draught?
>
> *15:18* But those things which proceed
> out of the mouth come forth from the
> (unawakened) heart; and they defile
> the man.
>
> — *Gospel of Matthew*

Many students report a loss of interest in television because their own interior television is suddenly going on so intensely.

# 6

# MEDITATE

Each day (a day means the time from dawn to sunset) find time and solitude for meditation—not at night but during the day, before the sun sets—between dawn and sunset. There is a reason for this, and again it has to do with biorhythms and earth cycles.

Most importantly, meditation in the late afternoon will allow unconscious material to erupt and clear Karmic patterns. Remember: meditation has been defined as "dreaming sitting up." You do not hesitate to press your PC reset button if something goes awry, and yet we never think to reset ourselves through meditation on a daily basis.

That "an ounce of prevention is worth a pound of cure" is a well-known saying, and I cannot emphasize strongly enough that the overwhelming evidence for the psychological and physiological benefits of meditation leads to the logical conclusion that meditation is the most positive and powerful prophylactic we have within our grasp.

There are a number of meditation methods, and you must find the one that suits you. However, be very careful that you do not become a meditation grasshopper. Once you find one that seems to fit—stick to it, cultivate it, make it your cocoon, make it your mobile shelter against the problems of the world, and realize that anything under twenty minutes a day is of no use!

The object of my meditation techniques, including the one I explain below, is to experience deep relaxation and resuscitation of the body and the inner being.

I cannot emphasize enough that these meditations are intended to provide a psychic and mental refuge that will allow you to restore yourself daily. Meditation should be a pleasure, not a strain, not work, not something you dread having to do as a duty. The two key criteria by which you can judge your progress in learning to relax into meditation are:

- The feeling that you are about to lose control of your neck muscles when you are sitting up

- The emergence of spontaneous dreams and visions, accompanied by the sensation of borderline sleep—yet you are not asleep

The ultimate goal of the techniques I teach is always refreshment of body and soul.

## Karma Shakti Kriya Meditation

This is a very beautiful way of meditating that involves synchronizing gently three aspects:

- Awareness of your spontaneous, uninhibited, uninterfered-with breath cycle of inhalation and exhalation.

- The mental repetition of the classic mantra "So Hum" with your breath cycle so that you silently

say "So" as your breath
flows spontaneously in,
and silently say "Hum" as
your breath flows out.

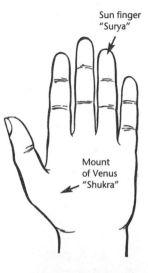

Sun finger
"Surya"

Mount
of Venus
"Shukra"

- The synchronized move-
  ment of the ring finger
  toward the fleshy mound
  at the base of your left
  thumb with the natural
  inhalation of your breath
  and the gentle movement
  of the finger away from
  the base of the thumb as
  your breath spontaneously
  flows out.

  With this technique you sit up comfortably,
cross-legged on a couch or in a chair, with your
feet comfortably supported by a cushion or folded
blanket on the floor. It is fine to have your back
supported, but leave your head free so you notice
when you begin to nod off—which, contrary to
what others tell you, is a good sign.

  Proceed to unite the movement of your left
ring finger with the inflow and outflow of your
breath and also harmonize the So Hum mantra.
This is a yoking of breath, body (finger
movement), and thought (mantra) which is
truly classical Yoga.

A summary of the technique is given on page 166:

1. When the breath naturally flows in, silently say "SO" and touch the tip of the left ring finger to the base of the thumb.

2. When the breath naturally flows out, silently say "HUM" and move the left ring finger away from the base of the thumb.

3. Be sure to let the breath flow naturally without force or control. Hear the "SO HUM" in your mind, and with your eyes closed visualize your finger touching the base of the thumb.

4. Ignore thoughts and let them pass—don't worry about them or focus on them. Just relax, let yourself drift and almost fall asleep—your head nodding will stop you from actually falling asleep. If the environment is noisy or if it will assist you to relax, have serene music playing in the background, and enjoy the experience!

The goal is *refreshment* through relaxing sitting up, dreaming sitting up, or sleeping sitting up. When you are conscious of yourself snoring, this is a special state.

This is a very special Karma Shakti Kriya that gently coaxes you into the beautiful interior depths of yourself. A variation of this Kriya was a favorite of the great Yogananda (founder of SRF) and his wonderful disciple, Swami Kriyananda.

The movement of the left ring finger "bowing" toward the mound of the thumb, and then withdrawing with the release of your breath, takes up immense slack in your mind and reduces agitation. Psychically, this is a very special thing I am asking you to do, and to understand this we need to consider an aspect of Indian Palmistry (some say palmistry originated in India).

The left ring finger is sacred to *Surya* (the creative power of the Sun—Apollo in Western palmistry) and very specifically to *Anahata Chakra* or the "Heart Center." The fleshy pad at the base of the thumb is known as *Shukra's mount,* or the mount of Venus. Symbolically, when you do this meditation you are opening your heart center to universal love, which is the alchemical solvent that dissolves Karma.

Notice that when you get very relaxed the breath may almost cease. Both Swami Gitananda and Yogananda taught that this *Kewali Kumbhaka,* or spontaneous cessation of breath, was a very positive sign of deep metabolic rest.

Be aware that the gentle to and fro movement of your ring finger may spontaneously cease also. If you feel yourself coming out of the meditation you can re-instigate the finger movement to take yourself back in. A full exposition of this technique may be found in my book *Death: Beginning or End?* (St. Paul: Llewellyn, 1999).

You may wish to browse through some of my earlier books for other meditations. My *Mind Magic Kit,* (Llewellyn, 1998) features a wholistic system suitable for everyone. The "Copper Meditation" in chapter 13 of *A Chakra & Kundalini Workbook,* (Llewellyn, 1994) and the "Chakra Stimulation with the Tattwa Cards" in chapter 6 of *Magical Tattwas* (Llewellyn, 1997) are also useful.

# ❧ 7 ❧
# DO SOMETHING DAILY THAT YOU NORMALLY DISLIKE

Once a day, do something you don't normally like doing and that it is not imperative to do.

That is the catch! There are things that we all don't like doing, but it is imperative that we do them. Some of us don't like going to work, but we like eating so we do go to work—that doesn't count.

You have got to do something that you don't like doing, but that is not essential to daily survival. In other words, you get to eat and drink without doing it. That makes an interesting challenge!

This is when we start to become conscious of how superficial our lives are—and this is when we can learn to become more conscious of our robotic *unconsciousness*. Deliberately and daily forcing ourselves to do something nonessential is the secret of developing *Itcha Shakti*, or will power!

Remember I said it is neither easy nor difficult. What we are engaged in with this Karma Kriya technique is *Spiritual Alchemy*, also referred to as *Transcendental Alchemy*.

> The alchemist's Lab Oratory is a temple of
> unceasing work (Karma Yoga) and prayer
> (Bhakti Yoga, i.e., love).
>
> — *Magical Tattwas*

# ❧ **8** ❧
# SELFLESS ACT

Each day seek an opportunity to do a selfless act that no one else knows about.

So you do something for someone else or something that is good for the Cosmos, but it is never identified with you. That is true detachment from the fruits of your actions!

We all enjoy doing things for other people that are recognized and observable, but when you do things and you are not allowed to let anyone else know about them, that hauls you up short on a psychic leash. The Karmic, spiritual effects of this exercise are profound.

A hint of this spiritual practice emerged in the mid-nineties with the lovely concept of *Random Acts of Kindness.*

# ❧ 9 ❧

# REVIEW AND RECALL

This is the night-time portion of the Kriya Shakti. The method is found independently in both Western and Eastern teachings. Pythagoras, by tradition, was said to advocate the practice, and quite recently, in 1995, Parahamsa Niranjan, the director of the Saraswati order, was teaching a variation of this method.

> For that inner spiritual truth has to do with
> the most difficult thing that many of us can
> come to—that is the truth to the Self,
> acknowledging the flaws, looking within and
> seeing what is there, facing it without fear,
> and going within
>
> — *A Chakra and Kundalini Workbook*

Let me explain. We are all very well aware that eating food is the beginning of a process. The fact that we put food in our mouths does not guarantee that we get benefit from it—never mind the quality of the food. So in order to get benefit from food, it must be digested and assimilated, that is, taken up into smaller molecules that can be absorbed by the liver and the bloodstream so that we can get our carbohydrates, proteins, and fats.

And thus it is with life. We can have an experience that bangs us right in the head, but it is like putting food in the mouth—we have not yet digested or assimilated that experience. The automatic Karmic procedure that attempts to assimilate our life experience in Western psychology we call dreaming. In Yoga it is known as *Swapna,* the "dreaming state."

Dreams are to our life experiences as digestion and assimilation are to the food we take in. It is through dreaming that we work out some of our Karma, we work out some of the experiences we have had, and we have a chance to assimilate and digest them. What we want to do is speed that up. This is the actual Kriya that reduces your Karmic storehouse—rather like emptying the recycle bin on your computer every night before leaving work.

What you do is get into bed and turn the lights out. Then with the lights out:

- Review Backward

    Review the entire day as if you were watching a video backwards. Start from the moment you climbed into bed and you start running the whole film in reverse. Getting into bed, brushing your teeth, right back through the day, and see if you can get to rising out of bed that morning.

    I will tell you what will happen. Some of you are insomniacs. The first few nights you try this you will fall into the deepest sleep because there will be so much resistance from your unconscious that it will decide "Oh we'll put her [or him] to sleep, this is getting serious." So you run the film backward, and as you run the film backward the next step is this.

- Pause and Experience

  When you notice an emotion attached to an experience, press the pause button (as you do on the video recorder) and experience that emotion. Note the details of the emotion as you recall the experience.

- Evaluate and Rectify

  You evaluate that experience and in the evaluation, make a decision about whether it could be rectified. Then you rectify that experience—just imagine it some other way, a more positive way for you.

  This is very interesting, because you are consciously utilizing visualization, implementation, and evaluation. Evaluation followed by rectification is the basis of Life Management skills, and by doing this part of the Karma Shakti routine you incorporate what quality assurance consultants call ongoing continuous improvement.

I have commented about the ramifications of visualization, implementation, and evaluation in chapter 7, "Shaping the Future," of *Magical Tattwas* (Llewellyn, 1997):

> This presupposes, of course, that we have the sense to establish priority goals, both short-term and long-term, for our life. A human without defined goals is like a ship without a navigator—or worse yet, a ship without a rudder! Without goal setting, we become

flotsam and jetsam upon the sea of life—and
we have only ourselves to blame!
 You review the day backwards and every time
you hit a memory that evokes an emotion you
press the pause button. You experience that
emotion, evaluate it, and in the world of
imagination, which is the ultimate world in which
things happen, you rectify it. Then you press
"start" on your internal video again, and go on.

The first few nights you are going to have the most
amazing experiences. You will find memories are coming up and banging into you. Some of you will fall
deeply asleep by the time you have remembered brush-
ing your teeth before getting into bed. Others of you
will find that as you are working through it, things from
childhood will come up that you haven't remembered
for twenty years. With anything that comes up while
you are doing this Karma Shakti Kriya, watch it, just
observe, just be the witness.

# frying the Seeds?

Now comes another question: This program is a window of opportunity opening in your life—will you take
the opportunity in this life?
 Black mustard seeds are a hallmark of South Indian
cooking. Mustard seeds may be planted with the resulting endless harvesting of future crops, or alternatively
they may be used in food preparation.

Mustard seeds fried in oil never sprout again—and in the deep-frying process they impart the most wonderful flavor to anything cooked with them.

When we fry the seeds of our Karma, the flavor of our life is enhanced and life should always be a journey to be savored—never a mere destination called death!

So now the question could be phrased: "If We Fry the Seeds?"

Let me tell you a famous fable illustrating the position at which you have arrived.

# The Guru and the Baby Bird

Once upon a time, in South India, there lived a very renowned Swami who could answer any questions asked of him. The man was truly amazing!

Whenever you approached him with a query, he would reply immediately. He could tell you if treasure was buried deep in your fields, what was on the other side of the moon, who you would marry, university exam results (before you even wrote the exam!), your promotion prospects in public service, how many children you would have—in short anything at all you wanted to know!

The soothsayer's reputation was known throughout India, and people came from all regions to receive his *darshan* (blessing) and ask advice.

Every morning at 8:00 A.M. the wise Swami would hold *Satsang* for devotees and seekers. At this time he would deal with questions or problems from the assembled throng.

One of the young men in the village became quite jealous of the Swami's omniscience and wisdom, especially since all the young women adored the Guru. South Indian girls are very pretty indeed!

This young man did not believe that any human could possibly be always *right*—and yet the Guru never seemed to be *wrong.* So the aspiring, conspiring youth decided that he would demonstrate publicly the guru's fallibility at a morning Satsang.

His scheme was to get a baby chick and hide it behind his back (with the little creature's beak firmly held shut by a thumb and forefinger to prevent any telltale "peep peep".

He would present himself before the Guru and ask the pandit what he had behind his back. If the Swami answered, "a chick," which would certainly be startling, the young man would immediately move into the second part of the plot by asking, "Is it alive or dead?"

If the Guru said "alive!" the young man would snap the chick's neck and, dangling the poor bird's corpse in front of the hopefully startled Guru and audience, would shout "You're wrong—it's dead!"

The lad thought long and carefully about his plan and became convinced that it was absolutely foolproof.

On the fateful day he waited patiently in line, and when his turn came, he asked loudly: "Gurujii, what is it I have behind my back?"

Quick as a flash, the Swami replied, "A baby chicken."

In response, our young man proclaimed "Swamijii, knower of all things in the ocean and sky—is the chick alive or dead?"

Even quicker than before came the reply: "It's in your hands!"

So now the real question is "Will you fry the seeds?"

# Frying the Seeds!

The best chance you have to achieve this program is the first time you try. If you can do this for nine days, you will experience nine days of amazing unconscious material—you will prevent Agami Karma from being watered and converted into Prarabdha Karma. Best of all you will emerge, like a butterfly from a cocoon, a more powerful, sensitive, insightful human with an increased sense of purpose, destiny, self-mastery, and satisfaction!

*Hari Om Tat Sat*

# APPENDIX

##  Study of Yoga

A note regarding the late Dr. Swami Maharishi Gitananda Giri's South Indian School. Swamijii founded Ananda Ashram upon a firm foundation of Ashtanga Yoga, plus a unique Kriya and Yoga therapy (Yoga Chikitsa).

Dr Swami Gitananda had his Mahasamadhi (transition) December 29, 1993. His successor is his son, Dr. Ananda, who is now completing his medical residency.

Each October, a six-month, live-in training course is commenced. This is one of the most intense courses in India. I often go over in February for a month to teach Yantra to the students. It is a very international group.

177

South Indian culture is totally different. An extra feature for Western students is an opportunity to study Bharat-Natyam and Carnatic vocal music with an integrated Yoga course.

The school is known as the International Center for Yoga Education and Research (ICYER). For further information, you may write to the director at the following address:

International Center for Yoga Education & Research
Yogacharini Meenakshi Devi Bhavanani, Director
16a 16b Mettu Street
Chinnamudaliarchavady
Kottakuppam 605104 (via Pondicherry)
Tamil Nadu
South India

# GLOSSARY

**Agami Karma:** Karma collected from birth onward; the seeds are there but not yet sprouted. It can be sprouted at any moment and is the result of inevitable action and reaction or consequences to things that we have done.

**Ahamkara:** The self-conscious mind in its unawakened, unrealized state; represented by Arjuna in the *Bhagavad Gita*.

**AMORC:** Rosicrucian Order founded in the 1920s by Dr. H. Spencer Lewis.

**Ananda:** Bliss, joy.

***Bhagavad Gita:*** Textbook of Karma Yoga; Yoga scripture in the form of a story, probably the most famous; an episode in one of the two national epics of India, the *Mahabharata* (the other national epic is the *Ramayana*).

**Bhakti:** Love; devotion; one of the methods to fry the seeds of SaBija and Agami Karma.

**Brahma:** The Hindu God of Creation; one of the classic triad; the first element and the *generation* part in the GOD process—Brahma, Vishnu, and Shiva— Generation, Order, and Disintegration.

**Bramacharya:** The educational and student phase of life; traditionally birth to twenty-five years of age; in Yantra (Indian Life Cycles) it is twenty-seven years of age.

**Buddha:** The founder of Buddhism.

**Buddhism:** The eightfold path consisting of correct vision, correct resolve, correct speech, correct conduct, correct livelihood, correct exertion, correct mindfulness, and correct concentration.

**Dharma:** The inherent individual responsibility each of us owes to the society of sentient beings we are born into, the environment and finally the higher "self" within us.

**Dharma Yuga:** The Life Cycle period; first Minor Dharma Yuga is the Brahmacharya Ashrama (educative period from zero to twenty-eight years); the Second Minor Dharma Yuga is the Grahasta Ashrama (productive period from twenty-eight to fifty-four years) and the third Dharma Yuga is the Vanaprastha Ashram (leisure period from age fifty-five to eighty-one).

**Dridha Karma:** Karma that is firm or fixed and is difficult or impossible to change so is destined to be experienced.

**Gestalt:** A Western form of therapy; a psychology technique.

**Grahastha:** The second life cycle period; the second Minor Dharma Yuga is the Grahasta Ashrama (Productive period from twenty-eight to fifty-four years).

**Hindu:** A follower or an aspect of Hinduism.

**Hinduism:** The dominant culture of India.

**Hutzpah:** A Jewish expression: outrageous "hide," nerve, verve.

**Jiwan Mukta:** He who is "free in life"; *Mukta* means free; *Jivan* means life.

**Kapila:** A contemporary of Buddha and the founder of Samkhya, one of the six classical schools of Indian philosophy.

**Karma:** The law of psycho-spiritual growth that involves an equal and opposite reaction for every action.

**Karma Shakti Kriya:** A powerful technique to burn off Karma equivalent to a deep-frying of the seeds in your being that represent potential SaBija and Agami Karma; designed by Dr. Swami Gitananda Giri.

**Kinetic Karma:** Parabdhra Karma; karma in full motion; when the seed is sprouted and the consequences are already clearly and irrevocably manifest.

**Krishna:** The charioteer and tutor of Arjuna in the *Bhagavad Gita*; Arjuna's supraconsciousness.

**Kurukshetra:** The battlefield in the *Bhagavad Gita*; the battlefield of life.

**Lila:** Chance; "Play of the Gods."

**Mahabharatha:** One of the two great national epics of India, the other is the Ramayana.

**Manu Matsya:** Law of creation that "big fish eat little fish."

**Maya:** Illusion; phantom existence; illusion of life.

**Numerology:** The science of form and numbers, life cycles; Yantra.

**Prarabdha Karma:** Karma that has already sprouted and nothing can stop it; the consequences are absolutely unavoidable (alt. spelling: Pararabdha).

**Patanjali:** The yoga authority who lived in the second century; the author of the Yoga Sutras.

**Rosicrucian:** AMORC; Order founded in the 1930s by Dr. H. Spencer Lewis.

**SaBija Karma:** Karma stored before and during birth; latent Karma; could also be called "Static Karma"; seeds waiting to be sprouted given the right stimulus and external environment.

**Samkhya:** One of the six classical schools of Indian philosophy developed by the sage Kapila about the universe and life; the theoretical basis on which the practice of Yoga rests; the Laws of the Universe, including Karma.

**Samsara:** Flow; the eternal bondage of rebirth; the cycle of life and death.

**Sannyasa:** Absolute renunciation of everything but God. May be taken at any time in life, but traditionally after eighty-one to the end of life.

**Sanskrit:** Ancient Indo-Germanic literary language of India.

**Saraswati:** Indian Goddess; the mistress of music and arts, and the bestower of wisdom; normally seen holding the Indian Lute (Veena).

**Sattvic:** Being; one of the three constituents of nature, Sattva (light), Rajas (mobile), and Tamas (inertia).

**Shakti:** Energy; Indian Goddess; female partner; personification of the divine; energy underlying manifest existence; the feminine counterpart of Shiva.

**Shankacharya:** The Hindu reformist who divided Karma into three categories.

**Shiva:** Consciousness; static; Indian God; personification of the divine masculine (the female being Shakti). Third part of the Hindu trinity—the *disintegration* part of the process we call Brahma, Vishnu, and Shiva: G(eneration), O(rder), and D(isintegration).

**Static Karma:** SaBija Karma; latent Karma stored before and during birth.

**Swadharma:** The innate psychic tendency or nature; Dharma as it applies to one's self.

**Teratogenic:** Congenital defects, i.e. those things acquired in the womb that affect us after birth.

**Transactional:** Transactional Analysis (T.A.); a theoretical framework and technique used by psychologists, designed by psychiatrist Eric Berne.

**Vanaprastha:** The third life cycle period; the third Dharma Yuga; leisure period from age fifty-five to eighty-one.

**Vedanta:** Esoteric body of literature; dominant philosophy of Hinduism.

**Vishnu:** Indian God; the *order* part of the process in Hinduism we call Brahma, Vishnu, and Shiva— G(eneration), O(rder) and D(isintegration).

**Yantra:** The science of form, numbers, name, and life cycles; one of the three mystic sciences of the East; the others are Tantra and Mantra.

# BIBLIOGRAPHY

Chaplin, J. P. *Dictionary of Psychology.* New York: Dell, 1985.

Gitananda Giri, Dr Swami (Yogamaharishi). *Yantra: the Mystic Science of Number, Name and Form.* Posthumous publication. Pondicherry, South India: ICYER, 1995.

Lewis, H. Spencer. *Mental Poisoning.* San Jose, CA: AMORC Books, 1987.

Mumford, Dr. Jonn. *A Chakra & Kundalini Workbook.* St. Paul: Llewellyn Publications, 1994.

———. *Death: Beginning or End?* St. Paul: Llewellyn Publications, 1999.

———. *Ecstasy Through Tantra.* St. Paul: Llewellyn Publications, 1987.

———. *Magical Tattwa Cards: A Complete System for Self-Development.* St. Paul: Llewellyn Publications, 1997.

———. *Mind Magic Kit.* St. Paul: Llewellyn Publications, 1998.

Rajmani, Tigunait Pandit PhD. *From Death to Birth, Understanding Karma and Reincarnation.* Honesdale, PA: The Himalayan Institute Press, 1997.

Svoboda, Robert E. *Ayurveda: Life, Health and Longevity.* Victoria, Australia: Penguin Books, 1992.

Svoboda, Robert E., and Hart Defouw. *Light On Life: An Introduction to the Astrology of India.* Victoria, Australia: Penguin Books, 1996.

*Teachings of Swami Satyananda.* Volume 1. Monghyr, India: Bihar School of Yoga, 1981.

Usha, Brahmacharini, Editor. *A Ramakrishna-Vedanta Wordbook: A Brief Dictionary of Hinduism.* Hollywood: Vedanta Press.

Watson, Lyall. *Beyond Supernature: A New Natural History of the Supernatural.* New York: Bantam, 1988.

Zimmer, Heinrich. *Philosophies of India.* Joseph Campbell, Editor. Princeton, NJ: Princeton University Press, 1969.

# INDEX

## O

Old Testament, 126

## P

Pandus, 121–122, 124, 126
Prarabdha Karma, 23, 49, 69–72, 78, 84, 176, 181–182
Patanjali, 26, 182
Pythagoras, 170

## R

Rabin, 51
Religion, 3, 123, 151
Ritual, 19–20, 28
Rosicrucian, 35, 80, 150, 179, 182

## S

SaBija Karma, 23–24, 33–41, 43, 48, 69, 77, 83–84, 136, 157, 182–183
Samkhya, 7–8, 181–182
Samsara, 24, 135, 183
Sannyasa, 54, 183

Sanskrit, 13, 19–21, 24, 49, 79, 107, 183
Saraswati, 170, 183
Sattvic, 97, 183
Satyananda, 154, 157, 186
Schiller, Friedrich, 17
Schweitzer, Albert, 120
Scorpion and the Turtle, 6
Shakespeare, 57
Shakti, 12, 91, 93, 127, 149–150, 153–154, 160, 164, 166, 168, 170, 172–173, 181, 183
Shankacharya, 23, 47, 84, 183
Shiva, 115, 127, 180, 183–184
Sin, 2, 142
Static Karma, 69, 182–183
Supernature, 35, 186
Svoboda, Robert, 57, 78, 141, 186
Swadharma, 5, 183
Swift, Jonathan, 123

# 🌙 REACH FOR THE MOON

*Llewellyn publishes hundreds of books on your favorite subjects! To get these exciting books, including the ones on the following pages, check your local bookstore or order them directly from Llewellyn.*

## ORDER BY PHONE

- Call toll-free within the U.S. and Canada, 1–800–THE MOON
- In Minnesota, call (651) 291–1970
- We accept VISA, MasterCard, and American Express

## ORDER BY MAIL

- Send the full price of your order (MN residents add 7% sales tax) in U.S. funds, plus postage & handling to:

   **Llewellyn Worldwide**
   **P.O. Box 64383, Dept. K490–1**
   **St. Paul, MN 55164–0383, U.S.A.**

## POSTAGE & HANDLING

(For the U.S., Canada, and Mexico)
- $4.00 for orders $15.00 and under
- $5.00 for orders over $15.00
- No charge for orders over $100.00

We ship UPS in the continental United States. We ship standard mail to P.O. boxes. Orders shipped to Alaska, Hawaii, The Virgin Islands, and Puerto Rico are sent first-class mail. Orders shipped to Canada and Mexico are sent surface mail.

**International orders: Airmail**—add freight equal to price of each book to the total price of order, plus $5.00 for each non-book item (audio tapes, etc.).

**Surface mail**—Add $1.00 per item.

**Allow 2 weeks for delivery on all orders.**
**Postage and handling rates subject to change.**

## DISCOUNTS

We offer a 20% discount to group leaders or agents. You must order a minimum of 5 copies of the same book to get our special quantity price.

**FREE CATALOG:** Get a free copy of our color catalog, *New Worlds of Mind and Spirit*. Subscribe for just $10.00 in the United States and Canada ($30.00 overseas, airmail). Many bookstores carry *New Worlds*—ask for it!

**Visit our web site at www.llewellyn.com for more information.**

*Access your psychic centers
with the Tattwas, the ancient Hindu
symbols of the five elements . . .*

# Magical Tattwa Cards

## A Complete System
## of Self-Development

### Dr. Jonn Mumford
(Swami Anandakapila Saraswati)

Tattwas—the ancient Hindu symbols of the five elements (earth, air, fire, water and ether)—act as triggers to the psychic layers of our mind through the combined power of their geometrical shapes and their vibrating primal colors. Tattwas are amazingly potent "psychic elevators" that can lift you to ever higher levels of mental functioning. The Hermetic Order of the Golden Dawn has used the tattwas for meditation, scrying, astral travel and talismans. Now, with this new kit, you can use the tattwas yourself for divination and for bringing yourself into altered states of consciousness.

The twenty-five tattwa symbols are printed on 4" x 4" cards in flashing colors (colors that when placed next to each other appear to flash or strobe). Although the geometrical shapes of the tattwas have long been an integral part of the Western Magical Tradition, the flashing colors and their divinatory aspects have never before been available as the complete integral system presented here.

MAGICAL TATTWA CARDS
1-56718-472-3, Boxed Set: 26 full-color cards
and 5³⁄₁₆ x 8, 288-pp. illustrated book          $29.95

# Mind Magic Kit

## Dr. Jonn Mumford
(Swami Anandakapila Saraswati)

The *Mind Magic Kit* is a dynamic program that gives you the ultimate combination of stress-management tools: fractional relaxation and autogenic temperature control. The kit includes an audio cassette, instruction book, and a hand-held biofeedback thermometer with which to gauge your progress.

Side one of the tape, "Fractional relaxation," guides you through a progressive relaxation that eliminates mental tension and cultivates life-affirming states of mind.

Side two of the tape, "Autogenic Training," is your gateway to thermal biofeedback (control of circulation in the hands and feet), voluntary control of your autonomic nervous system, and meditation. It uses a simple trigger word as a mantra, which when silently repeated will lead you into the interior depths of yourself.

Practice the autogenic temperature control techniques provided in this kit and increase the temperature in your hands and feet at will; learn the secret key code word that will move you quickly into deep meditative states; alleviate psychosomatic illness; increase secretion of the pineal hormone melatonin to reverse aging, fight cancer, and rejuvenate energy; learn to master anxiety, nervousness, migraines, Raynaud's disease, and insomnia; improve concentration skills, and relaxation response; reduce and ultimately eliminate mental tension and stress; and cultivate life-affirming states of mind

**MIND MAGIC KIT**
**1-56718-475-8, Boxed Kit: audiotape, 5³⁄₁₆ x 8,**
**96-pp. booklet, Biofeedback thermometer**     **$15.95**

**To Order, Call 1–800–THE MOON**
Prices subject to change without notice

# Ecstasy Through Tantra

## Dr. Jonn Mumford

(Swami Anandakapila Saraswati)

Dr. Jonn Mumford makes the occult dimension of the sexual dynamic accessible to everyone. One need not go up to the mountaintop to commune with Divinity: its temple is the body, its sacrament the communion between lovers. *Ecstasy Through Tantra* traces the ancient practices of sex magick through the Egyptian, Greek, and Hebrew forms, where the sexual act is viewed as symbolic of the highest union, to the highest expression of Western sex magick.

Dr. Mumford guides the reader through mental and physical exercises aimed at developing psychosexual power; he details the various sexual practices and positions that facilitate "psychic short-circuiting" and the arousal of Kundalini, the Goddess of Life within the body. He shows the fundamental unity of Tantra with Western Wicca, and he plumbs the depths of Western sex magick, showing how its techniques culminate in spiritual illumination. Includes 14 full-color photographs.

ECSTASY THROUGH TANTRA
0-87542-494-5, 6 x 9, 190 pp.,
14 color plates, softcover

$16.00

# Audiotapes

## Dr. Jonn Mumford

### Autoerotic Mysticism

Learn how to get in touch with yourself using massage. Focused autoerotic activity will lead to control and deep understanding of your sexual nature.

0–87542–514–3                                    **$9.95**

### Psychic Energizer

This is a mental reconditioning tape, utilizing both Western and Eastern techniques of tension release and fractional relaxation. Introduced and then narrated by Mumford, with special musical effects for deep psychic response.

0–87542–547–X                                    **$9.95**

### Sexual Tantra: Is It Possible?

Sexual Tantra, the creation and reenactment of the cosmos, of consciousness and matter—is it likely to happen? Dr. Mumford answers this question by exploring the nature of male/female relationships, feminism, and what men and women really desire.

0–87542–549–6                                    **$9.95**

### Tantric Sexuality

Dr. Mumford introduces concepts of sexuality in Tantra. Some concepts are new to the Western mind. Runner-up for Audio World's "Best Self-Help Tape of 1989."

0–87542–546–1                                    **$9.95**